Jean-Pierre de Caussade on reaching holiness by abandoning one's soul to God:

"In reality, holiness consists of one thing only: complete loyalty to God's will."

"Perfection is neither more nor less than the soul's faithful cooperation with God."

"Our only satisfaction must be to live in the present moment as if there were nothing to expect beyond it."

"You are seeking for secret ways of belonging to God, but there is only one: making use of whatever he offers you."

"If we only have sense enough to leave everything to the guidance of God's hand we should reach the highest peak of holiness."

"The great and firm foundation of the spiritual life is the offering of ourselves to God and being subject to his will in all things."

"The truly faithful soul accepts all things as a manifestation of God's grace, ignores itself and thinks only of what God is doing."

"Let us love, for love will give us everything."

"If we are truly docile, we will ask no questions about the road along which God is taking us."

"God truly helps us however much we may feel we have lost his support."

"The more God takes from the abandoned soul, the more is he really giving it . . . the more he strips us of natural things, the more he showers us with supernatural gifts."

"To all his faithful souls, God promises a glorious victory over the powers of the world and of hell."

ABANDONMENT
TO
DIVINE PROVIDENCE

Jean-Pierre de Caussade

Translated with an Introduction by
John Beevers

IMAGE
NEW YORK

CONTENTS

INTRODUCTION

In the sixteenth and seventeenth centuries France was rich in spiritual writers. Great names glow from the history of those centuries, and very rightly, for they are a vibrant part of the fabric of European civilization. But amongst these great names is one of a man who knew no public honor then, yet now has drawn to himself a deeper love than has attached itself to many who once shone like stars. He was Jean-Pierre de Caussade, a dim, shadowy figure about whom we know almost nothing. No painting or drawing of him exists. We do not know if he was tall or short, fat or thin. Was he bald? Had he blue or brown eyes? Was his voice high-pitched or low? Was he elegant or shabby? Shabby, I would imagine, but we just do not know. What we do know is this: He was born on March 6, 1675, but where is not certain. His birthplace was somewhere in the province of Quercy in the south of France, and it seems fairly certain that he spent his childhood in the town of Cahors to the north of Toulouse, a town which then had a flourishing university. Twenty years before, Fénelon was a student there. In 1693, Caussade became a Jesuit novice in Toulouse, was ordained priest in 1704, and took his final vows four years later. During this time he was never in one place for very long: he taught Greek and Latin at Auch and Aurillac, was professor of philosophy at Rodez, and later held the same post at Mauriac and Albi. None of these towns is very far from Toulouse, and it was back to the university there that he went for his theological studies and took his doctorate in theology. Then, until 1720, Caussade resumed his teaching in various towns, but in that year he ceased the life of a professor and was sent as preacher and confessor to many places in southern and central France. In 1729, he arrived in the splendid city of Nancy, the former capital of the Dukes of Lorraine in the northeast corner of France. It was a momentous event in the history of spirituality, for he became the director of the Visitation nuns in their

Nancy convent, with the consequences we shall see. He stayed there for just over a year, returned to Toulouse and went to Albi. He returned to Nancy at the end of 1733 and remained for nearly six years. He next appears as Rector of the Jesuit College in Perpignan, and then of the College in Albi. The last five years of his life were spent as director of the theological students in the Jesuit House in Toulouse. He died in 1751 at the age of seventy-six.

The little we know about him is contained in the letters he wrote to the nuns of Nancy—and that could be put on a couple of postcards, for his letters are concerned with spiritual matters. They are not the letters of a Horace Walpole. But from one or two paragraphs it is clear that he did not live a sheltered life, cut off from the business of the great world. When, for example, he was transferred from Nancy to Perpignan, he wrote to Sister Marie-Thérèse at Nancy: "When I arrived in Perpignan, there was a mass of business— of which I understood nothing—waiting for me to tackle, and a great many people I had to see and try to settle their differences: the Bishop, the Governor, the King's Lieutenant, the Army Staff and members of Parliament. You know how much I detest any formal visits—especially those involving the great figures of the world, yet I found that none of this worried me. I feel such confidence in God that I rise above all these troubles and remain at peace when I should have expected to have been completely overwhelmed by this multitude of complicated affairs."

And, to the same nun, a little later: "At first I suffered greatly under a load of business worries, which of course are wholly at variance to my love of silence and solitude. But God came to my aid and gave me the grace to stay quite uninvolved in all these affairs. My spirit stays free. I am not plagued by many visitors, because I myself pay visits only when duty and sheer necessity make them essential. My fellow Jesuits, who know my feelings, finish their business with me as soon as possible. They are well aware that it is not pride or misanthropy which make me shun society, so not one of them objects to my behavior and some of them even appear edified by it."

To another nun, Sister Marie-Antoinette, he wrote: "Here

I am back in Albi with its lovely climate and its charming people. They have only one fault: I love solitude and they are so friendly. I shall get many invitations and they will be a real cross to me, and no doubt God will send me others to stop me from taking too much pleasure in the beauties of a countryside I have always loved."

But Albi had other pleasures apart from the beauty of its landscapes to offer Caussade. In a letter to one of the Visitation nuns, he tells her that he has "discovered something which gives me infinitely more satisfaction than anything you can imagine. Here in Albi there is a convent of Poor Clares who are completely cut off from the world. They enter religion without any dowry and live entirely on alms. Their superior is the holiest person I have ever met . . . I have never known such gaiety and holy joy as among these saintly nuns . . . what a grace and comfort for me and what an example for my own sanctification!"

This is all that can be dredged up from the past about Caussade, apart from the fact that he published one book, and that anonymously. Its title: *Spiritual Instructions in the form of Dialogues concerning different Methods of Prayer according to the teaching of M. Bossuet, Bishop of Meaux, by a Father of the Company of Jesus.* It is not an outstanding book in any way and would long ago have been forgotten were it not for his second book, which appeared a hundred and ten years after his death: *Abandonment to Divine Providence.* He never knew he had written this second book. It is a strange story. During the years he spent in Nancy he was, as we have seen, the spiritual director of the Visitation nuns there. He wrote many letters to them and gave them conferences, and they preserved his letters and the notes of these conferences. What superb eighteenth-century French names these sisters had: Charlotte-Elisabeth Bourcier de Monthu-ieux, Marie-Antoinette de Mahuet de Lupcourt, Anne-Marguerite Boudet de la Bellière. And there were two sisters: Marie-Anne-Thérèse de Rosen and Louise-Françoise de Rosen, daughters of a Marshal of France. Louise-Françoise was four times elected superior of the convent, and she and her sister took particular care to preserve all that came from the pen of Caussade. There was also a niece of these two sisters, Marie-

Anne-Sophie de Rottembourg, who also served several terms
as superior. She was novice mistress when Caussade first went
to Nancy. A letter from him to her forms the first two sections of the first chapter of *Abandonment* and part of the
third section, and it is in this way that the book was formed.
During the last century some of Caussade's letters to sisters
and superiors, and notes taken of talks he gave to them during
retreats, were handed to a learned French Jesuit, Fr. Henri
Ramière, who assembled and edited them into a small volume
which was published in 1861. It at once found many read-
ers. New editions appeared, and in them Fr. Ramière incorporated fresh material, until at last the book was as we have
it now. New editions continue to be published and it has
been translated into several languages.

A great master of the spiritual life, Dom John Chapman,
one-time Abbot of the English Benedictine Abbey of Down-
side, declared more than forty years ago: "For the last few
years I confess that I have found no writer so helpful to me
as Father Jean-Pierre de Caussade, of the Society of Jesus."
It has been said that Caussade is certainly among the ten
most significant spiritual guides of the last few centuries and
that the message of his book can be compared to that of the
Spiritual Canticles of St. John of the Cross and the Dialogues
of St. Catherine of Genoa. These are high tributes. Are they
deserved?

Abandonment to Divine Providence is a passionate book,
as are all great books. It can be a purely intellectual passion,
a sexual one, or a tremendous interest and delight in the
infinite complexities of human beings. The passion may be
controlled and hidden, turbulent and open, but it is always
there. Caussade's passion was both rational and emotional: it
was the adoration of God. The more one studies him, the
more difficult it becomes to imagine a single moment of his
life when he was not loving God. He had, of course, as we
have seen, a busy life. He was a very active priest and much
involved in the world, though very reluctantly. But he suc-
ceeded in keeping worldly affairs at arm's length and yet
making use of them. In one of his letters he declares:
"Everything helps me to him." And that is a cardinal principle of his. All things are sent and governed by God, and,

however troublesome they are, they will, if accepted gladly, lead us surely and quickly toward holiness.

Abandonment is a short book. Short books often have great power. A few that come to mind are Thomas à Kempis's *The Imitation of Christ*, the *Communist Manifesto*, Paine's *The Rights of Man*, Rousseau's *Social Contract*, St. Thérèse's *The Story of a Soul*, and, of course, the Gospels. There is a very human reason for this. Most people have neither the time nor the inclination to plough through a five-volume treatise. They want the message, whatever it is, given to them in as few pages as possible. This is no new phenomenon. Pamphlets may not give as much enjoyment as a many-volumed book, but it is arguable that they have had vastly more influence. And it is not only the reader who is affected by a short book. Its writer is. The effort, whether conscious or not, to concentrate his thought in a hundred or so pages instead of a thousand, gives this thought a sharpness and urgency which would inevitably be diffused over many volumes.

Although Caussade was a Jesuit and held several important posts within the Society, his teaching owes far more to Salesian and Carmelite spirituality than to that of St. Ignatius. It would, of course, have been impossible for him not to have come under the influence of St. Francis de Sales, for it was St. Francis and St. Jane de Chantal who, in 1610, founded the Visitation Order, and it was as a spiritual director of Visitation nuns that Caussade spent several years of his life. In any case, St. Francis was canonized only twenty years before Caussade was born, and his two masterpieces, *Introduction to the Devout Life* and *Treatise on the Love of God*, had gone into edition after edition, and it would have been impossible for a man such as Caussade not to have read them and realized how similar were his spiritual views and those of St. Francis.

Where Caussade says "abandonment," St. Francis generally uses the word "indifference," but this is merely a matter of vocabulary. St. Francis tells us to "ask for nothing and refuse nothing," and declares that "the indifferent heart is like a lump of wax in God's hands, readily receiving every impression of his will." He describes as a sure sign that we are truly and perfectly indifferent if we stop in the middle of some

meritorious work if God wills it and turn back halfway toward
a worthy goal if he says we should. Another word used by St.
Francis is "detached": "The detached soul does not care if
it is serving God by meditating, or serving him by looking
after a neighbor. What matters is what God wants the soul
to do at that particular time." We shall see how Caussade
expands this into his doctrine of "the duty of the present
moment"—a vital part of his spirituality.

But it is equally certain that the great Carmelite mystic
and doctor of the Church, St. John of the Cross, had a profound influence on Caussade. St. John was canonized just
three years before Caussade went for the first time to Nancy
and the Visitation convent there; and, as we know, there is
always a great flare-up of interest in the works and writings
of a man or a woman who is soon to be marked with the seal
of the Church as a person of surpassing holiness.

It is true that Caussade refers only once to St. John in
the letters of direction he wrote to his Visitation nuns, but
there is nothing unusual in that, for, though he must have
had a well-stocked mind, he very rarely makes use of quota-
tions. Even his use of Scripture is very limited. Yet how
often he echoes St. John of the Cross. The Carmelite declares that the soul must be like a blind man, enveloped in
the total darkness of faith and yet finding in this darkness
light and a sure guide. And over and over again, Caussade
insists: "There is nothing safer and less likely to lead us
astray than the darkness of faith . . . the very darkness acts
as our guide." We have St. John declaring: "In this life we cannot achieve union with God through our intellect, our imagination, or, indeed, through any of our senses. We can achieve
this union by faith, by hope and by love." What does Caussade say? "The state of self-abandonment is a blending of
faith, hope and love in one single act which unites us to God
and all his activities." One could fill many pages with cross-
references linking St. John and Caussade. But what I find
much more interesting is not the influence a Carmelite saint
had on this Jesuit father, but the influence this Jesuit had
on an equally great Carmelite saint, St. Thérèse of the Child
Jesus. St. Thérèse was born in 1873. Caussade's book was
first published in 1861, and many editions followed. What

ABANDONMENT TO DIVINE PROVIDENCE 13

I write now is pure supposition, but it may contain the truth.
St. Thérèse's family were devout and read a great number
of spiritual books. Is it not likely that Caussade's book was
one of them? But even if St. Thérèse's father, M. Martin,
did not ponder over it in his upstairs study at Les Buissonets,
the family home in Lisieux, it is hardly conceivable tha⁺ its
doctrine did not water and refresh the whole body of those
Catholics eagerly seeking holiness. For the most able modern
authority on Caussade, Father Olphe-Galliard, S.J., has made
very clear the great influence Caussade had on theologians—
who were also writers—at the end of last century. Thus it is,
I should say, more than likely that the saint heard of self-
abandonment in sermons and through her confessors. It must
be remembered, too, that for ten years she kept in close touch
with Father Almire Pichon, a Jesuit who became her spiritual
director when she was fourteen, and had been the friend and
confessor of the Martin family for many years. He was later
to go to Canada, but St. Thérèse kept in touch with him by
letter. She wrote her last letter to him a month before she
died: "My whole soul was in it," she said. But Father Pichon
destroyed all her letters—a strange act. And I express myself moderately. But I imagine that this Jesuit father was not
ignorant of Caussade, and I imagine, too, that his knowledge
of this eighteenth-century priest filtered through to St.
Thérèse. But it is time we finished with suppositions and
imaginings. Let us look at the evidence.

St. Thérèse always insisted that it was not the splendor
or the greatness of our deeds that mattered. The smallest,
most trivial task we accomplish is supremely important if it
is done in obedience to God's will and for love of him. Everything we do is judged by him according to the love which
inspires us. She declares that we can all perform such deeds,
for every one of us is capable of such love. More than two
hundred years earlier, Caussade said: "To achieve the height
of holiness, people must realize that all they count as trivial
and worthless is what can make them holy . . . consider your
life and you will see it consists of countless trifling actions.
Yet God is quite satisfied with them, for doing them as they
should be done is the part we have to play in our striving
for perfection."

Back to St. Thérèse. She told a lay sister: "Your life is one that is humble and hidden, but remember that nothing is small in the eyes of God. Do all that you do with love."

On her deathbed, she was asked what, after her death, she would teach all the souls who turned to her. She said at once that she would urge them to embark on "the way of spiritual childhood, the path of confidence and complete abandon." And in her autobiography, in that last chapter addressed to her sister, Marie, in which she says she will tell the "secrets Jesus has entrusted" to her, her words are: "Jesus never manifests himself nor lets me hear his voice. He teaches me in secret, but he has shown me the only path which leads to the divine furnace of his love. It is the complete abandonment of a baby sleeping without fear in its father's arms . . . Jesus does not demand great deeds. All he wants is self-surrender and gratitude . . . O Jesus, if only I could tell all *little* souls of your immeasurable condescension! I feel that if you found a soul feebler than mine—though that's impossible—you would delight in heaping even greater favors on it if it abandoned itself with supreme confidence to your infinite mercy."

When we come to consider Caussade's insistence upon what he calls "the sacrament of the present moment," we may think of St. Thérèse's words: "If I did not simply live from one moment to the next, it would be impossible for me to keep my patience. I can see only the present, I forget the past and I take good care not to think about the future. We get discouraged and feel despair because we brood about the past and the future. It is such folly to pass one's time fretting, instead of resting quietly on the heart of Jesus."

The whole purpose of St. Thérèse's Little Way is to convince men and women that they can become holy by abandoning themselves, without the slightest reserve, to God's will, and that he needs nothing from them "except our love." She calls St. Cecilia her favorite saint: "What especially delighted me was her abandonment to God and her boundless confidence in him." Abandonment and confidence—those are the two key words in St. Thérèse's teachings.

Now let us look at Caussade. His insistence on the supreme importance of abandonment has nothing new about it. How could it? Caussade was a Christian and the words of Jesus were with him always. "You must love the Lord your God with all your heart, with all your soul and with all your mind. This is the greatest and the first commandment." Centuries later, the teacher of St. Thomas Aquinas, St. Albert the Great, urged all Christians: "Commit every particle of your being in all things, down to the smallest details of your life, eagerly and with perfect trust to the unfailing and most sure providence of God." Similar exhortations can be found in the writings and sermons of nearly every saint. So, in this matter, Caussade was preaching no novel spiritual doctrine. He was, however, being courageous, for in the year he was born, 1675, there was published in Rome a book called *The Spiritual Guide*, written by a Spanish priest, Miguel de Molinos, who had settled in Rome a few years earlier. He was befriended by Pope Innocent XI and given an apartment in the Vatican. When his book appeared, it was prefaced by the warm approval of five high ecclesiastics, one a Jesuit and four Inquisitors. In five years it went into twenty editions in four languages. Its teaching swept Italy, and thousands adopted it as the basis of their spirituality. Put most briefly and inadequately, Molinos' teaching is that there are two kinds of religious life. One is the external one, and those who follow it seek God through their reason and imagination and by means of abstinence and mortification of the senses. They try to visualize God—as a pastor, a physician, a father or a lord. "They delight in continually speaking of God, very often making fervent acts of love. By this method they desire to be great. This is the external way and the way of beginners, and though it be good, yet by it there is no arriving at perfection, as experience shows in the case of many who, after fifty years of this external exercise, are void of God and full of themselves, having nothing of spiritual men but just the name of such." But there are others who live an internal life, those "withdrawn into the inner parts of their souls, resigning themselves wholly into the hands of God and going with an uplifted spirit into the presence of the Lord, by the means of pure faith, without image, form or figure, but with great assurance, founded in tranquillity and inner rest." Molinos does, of course, go into great detail about this internal spiritual life—to the extent of about a hundred and fifty pages of fairly small print. And it is a great and moving book. But it put Molinos in a cell for life.

Human beings are often all too human, and many who read Molinos saw what he taught as an easy way of salvation. Anyone, they thought, could practice contemplation, never realizing that to reach the state when contemplation becomes union with God requires a long and most arduous journey. And these mistaken souls took the view that by spending hours in what they wrongly believed to be contemplation they thereby absolved themselves from the normal practices of religion and from all those duties of charity demanded of a Christian. They became, in their own view, so spiritual that they threw away—literally—all the physical helps to devotion: rosaries, statues, pictures and relics. It was also easy to distort some of his teaching about temptation and the relative unimportance of much of human activity, so that it appeared highly dangerous both to the soul and to the social order.

In fact, Molinos was wrong on only two points. He declared that those who lead the internal spiritual life need not prepare themselves by confessing before receiving Holy Communion, for "their life is a continual and perfect preparation." Molinos himself went for twelve years without making his confession. This was, of course, for a Catholic, both wrong doctrine and wrong behavior.

His second error was his teaching that meditation was only for spiritual beginners and that it must be discarded and replaced by contemplation by those seeking to lead a Christian life at its highest level. While both methods are good, experience shows that souls seeking God are impelled by him to the one he knows is best suited to them. It was presumptuous—if not heretical—for Molinos to pronounce one way more efficacious than the other.

It is true he was writing for an educated and sophisticated public, one very knowledgeable about the language of mysticism. But it must always be remembered that there have been countless souls to whom the words "meditation" and "contemplation" have no meaning at all, and yet these souls have found God. There are a thousand ways to him.

Molinos was attacked by the Jesuits. It is a sordid story and a disgraceful episode in the history of the Church. It is a long and complicated one. All I need say here is that Molinos, on the orders of the Inquisition in Rome, was jailed in 1685. He stayed in prison for two years, during which the Inquisition made a thorough investigation of his book and his sermons and of the activities of his followers—two hundred of whom were flung into prison at the beginning of 1687. In the summer of that year, a decree of the Inquisition said Molinos had taught and practiced heretical doctrines, and it listed sixty-eight propositions drawn from his work and those of his followers. They were "heretical, blasphemous, offensive to pious ears, insolent, dangerous to and destructive of Christian morality."

Molinos was sentenced to imprisonment for life in a Dominican monastery after a great public ceremony during which he knelt and abjured all heresy. He died, still a prisoner, in 1697.

The heresy of which Molinos was found guilty was and is known as *Quietism*, and Caussade has been accused of drawing very near to it. It is true that *Abandonment to Divine Providence* was not published until long after he was dead, but he did preach what is now in print and he did write a great number of letters which carry the same message as his book. And he was a member of the Society of Jesus, the most implacable enemy of Quietism—and he was a subject of Louis XIV, who exerted full diplomatic pressure in Rome to secure the condemnation of Molinos.

Caussade is careful to dissociate himself from Quietism, saying that it is quite wrong when it condemns making use of books, advice and vocal prayer and employing our senses. He very rightly points out that God intends some people to use these means to help them on their way to him.

If we read Molinos and then Caussade, we shall inevitably be struck by a similarity in their thought. But there is an original, ever-present and dominant idea in Caussade which must destroy any belief that he had any sympathy with Quietism.

This idea is that of "the sacrament of the present moment." Like many ideas, it is a most obvious one—the moment we learn of it. It is simply this: most of us are very ordinary creatures with humdrum lives, work to be done, and with every day filled with a multiplicity of trivial decisions and tasks. Our lives are made up of a stream of petty affairs, some pleasant, many boring, and a lot unpleasant and often tragic. We must not exaggerate. There is a great deal of pleasure, even delight, in life. But there is also much that is irritating and tedious. Caussade says that everything in life is to be welcomed as the expression of the will of God, so we must "accept what we very often cannot avoid, and endure with love and resignation things which could cause us weariness and disgust. This is what being holy means." And "for most people the best way to achieve perfection is to submit to all that God wills for their particular way of life." Caussade tells us: "God speaks to every individual through what happens to them moment by moment." He goes on: "The events of each moment are stamped with the will of God . . . we find all that is necessary in the present moment." Again: "We are bored with the small happenings around us, yet it is these trivialities—as we consider them—which would do marvels for us if only we did not despise them." A key sentence in Caussade is: "If we have abandoned ourselves to God, there is only one rule for us: the duty of the present moment."

He insists, over and over again, that we must live from minute to minute. The past is past, the future is yet to be. There is nothing we can do about either, but we can deal with what is happening moment by moment. We must realize that there is nothing at all which happens unless willed by God, and our all-important duty is to co-operate with that will. Every act, every thought of every second, is significant. He does not mean that we must approach God before every snap decision we are forced to make. That would be absurd and impossible. But what he does mean is that we should have so completely abandoned ourselves to God that we are fully aware of what hangs upon every moment and that we react, as best we can, in the way God wishes.

Caussade combines intense practicality with profound mysticism—as did St. Teresa of Avila. This is nothing extraordinary. True mystics are always much more practical than the ordinary run of people. They seek reality; we, the ephemeral. They want God as he is; we want God as we imagine him to be.

Caussade was a very simple man. He was obsessed by one thought: the necessity of loving God and surrendering ourselves to him completely. If we love God we cannot go wrong. But what is original about him is that he said we need do no extraordinary works, show no unique devotion, behave in no uncommon manner. All we must do is our Christian duty continually. Nothing must be too paltry for us. The meanest incident must be seen as willed by God and must be dealt with as such. This attention to apparent trivialities will bring us as close to God as is possible during our life on earth and ensure that we shall enjoy complete union in the eternal life that awaits us.

I think that, at the first reading, Caussade should be gone through at one sitting to get the general idea he is driving at. Afterwards, give him several slow and careful readings. Then I believe that it will be realized that one is handling a masterpiece of spirituality, a short, intense book, highly charged with love and passion—love for you, the reader, as well as for God. For Caussade cares deeply for us. He is not interested in himself, but he is profoundly concerned about our eternal well-being. This concern breaks through every paragraph of his well-mannered eighteenth-century French. He adores God and loves us. He wants us to share his peace and joy. If we pay attention to him, we may.

JOHN BEEVERS

CHAPTER I

ON DOING OUR PART AND LEAVING
THE REST TO GOD

(1) *The holiness of the Old Testament saints, and indeed that of St. Joseph and the Blessed Virgin, came through their absolute obedience to God's will.*

Today God still speaks to us as he used to speak to our ancestors at a time when there were neither spiritual directors nor any systems of spirituality. To be faithful to the designs of God then comprised the whole of one's spiritual life. Religious devotion had not become a science crammed with precepts and detailed instructions. Nowadays, no doubt, our special needs make this necessary, but in the old days people were less complex and more straightforward. Then they knew only that each moment brought a duty which must be faithfully fulfilled. Those spiritually inclined needed nothing more. They were like the hand of a clock which, minute by minute, crosses its appointed space, for, ceaselessly prompted by divine grace, they attended without thinking to each new task offered them by God at every hour of the day.

This was the hidden motive of Mary's behavior. She was the simplest of humans and the one who made the most complete surrender of herself to God. Her laconic reply to the angel—"Let what you have said be done to me" (Luke 1:38)—embodies all the mystical theology of her ancestors. This, then as now, meant the most direct and wholehearted surrender to God's will, however it revealed itself. This noble and exalted frame of mind was the basis of Mary's spiritual life and reveals itself perfectly in those very simple words: "Let what you have said be done to me." We should note that they are in perfect agreement with those our Lord wants us to have always on our lips and in our hearts: "Your will be done" (Matt. 6:10). It is true that what was demanded of Mary at this great moment was something most glorious, but all its splendor would have meant nothing to her unless she had wanted to yield to the will of God. It was this will which governed all she did and thought. No matter what her jobs were—ordinary, commonplace, or seemingly more important ones—they revealed to her, sometimes quite clearly, sometimes obscurely, the activity of the Almighty and were an opportunity for her to praise God. Filled with joy, she regarded everything she had to do or suffer at any moment of her life as a gift from him who showers delights upon those who hunger and thirst only for him and not for the things of the world.

(2)   *The duties of each moment are shadows which hide the action of the divine will.*

The angel told Mary: "The power of the Most High will cover you with its shadow" (Luke 1:35). Now this shadow is whatever duty, temptation, or trial that every moment presents to us. It is exactly like those natural shadows which veil and hide objects from our sight. These ever-present duties conceal the fact that they are expressions of the divine will. That is how Mary always saw them; so, far from being deceived by them, she had her faith strengthened in him who never changes. The archangel departs, for he is one of these shadows. He has had his moment. Mary has gone ahead of him and henceforth a great distance will separate them, but the Holy Spirit, who came upon her under the shadow of the archangel, will never leave her.

There is very little unusual about the outward life of the Blessed Virgin, or at least the Gospels do not record it. They show her life as very simple and ordinary. What she did and endured might have been done and endured by anyone in her station of life. She visited her cousin Elizabeth just as her other relatives did. Like all her neighbors, she went to Bethlehem to be registered. Because she was poor she sheltered in a stable. The persecution of Herod drove her from Nazareth, but she returned and lived there with Jesus and

Joseph, who worked to earn their daily bread. But what was the bread which nourished the faith of Mary and Joseph? It was the sacrament of the moment. But what did they experience beneath an existence apparently filled with nothing but humdrum happenings? On the surface it was similar to that of everyone around them, but faith, piercing the superficialities, disclosed that God was accomplishing very great things. O bread of angels, heavenly manna, pearl of the Gospels, sacrament of the present moment! you give God under such lowly forms as the stable, the manger, the hay and the straw. But to whom do you give him? "The hungry he hath filled with good things" (Luke 1:53). God reveals himself to the humble in the lowliest of disguises, but the proud, who never look below the surface, fail to find him even in his greatest manifestations.

(3)   *How easy it is to be holy.*

If the business of becoming holy seems to present insufferable difficulties, it is merely because we have a wrong idea about it. In reality, holiness consists of one thing only: complete loyalty to God's will. Now everyone can practice this loyalty, whether actively or passively.

To be actively loyal means obeying the laws of God and the Church and fulfilling all the duties imposed on us by our way of life. Passive loyalty means that we lovingly accept all that God sends us at each moment of the day. Now is there anything here too difficult for us? Certainly nothing in active loyalty, for if its duties are beyond our powers, we are not expected to attempt to fulfill them. If we are too ill to go to Mass, we need not. And it is the same for all other precepts which lay down duties. But, of course, there can be no exemption from precepts which forbid wrongdoing, for we are never allowed to sin. Can anything be more sensible? Or easier? We are left without any excuse. Yet God asks nothing more than this. But he does require it from everyone, without exception. Class, time and place mean nothing. Everyone must obey. Yet all he is asking from us is very straightforward and quite easy. We can become truly holy by obeying these simple rules. However, apart from the Commandments, he gives us counsels of perfection; yet, even here, he takes care that the practice of them fits in with our temperament and our position in life. He never drives anyone beyond his strength or ability. What could be fairer?

God has compelled me to write this to help you who seek to be holy and are discouraged by what you have read in the lives of saints and some books dealing with spiritual matters. So do, please, try to learn from me.

God, who is all goodness, has made easily available for all the things necessary for life, such as earth, air and water. And what could be more vital than breathing, eating and sleeping? And what is easier? When we turn to spiritual matters, love and loyalty are just as vital, so they cannot be as difficult to acquire as we imagine. Consider your life, and you will see that it consists of countless trifling actions. Yet God is quite satisfied with them, for doing them as they should be done is the part we have to play in our striving for perfection. There can be no doubt about this. Holy Scripture makes it very plain: "Fear God, and keep his commandments, since this is the whole duty of man" (Eccles. 12:13). This is all we have to do. This is active loyalty. If we do our part, God will do the rest. Grace will pour into us and will perform marvels far beyond our understanding, for "no eye has seen and no ear has heard things beyond the mind of man, all that God has prepared for those who love him" (I Cor. 2:9). To be passively loyal is even easier, since it implies only that we accept what very often we cannot avoid, and endure with love and resignation things which could cause us weariness and disgust. Once again, this is what being holy means. It is the mustard seed which is almost too small to be recognized or harvested, the drachma of the Gospels, the treasure that no one finds, as it is thought to be too well hidden to be looked for.

But what is the secret of finding this treasure? There isn't one. This treasure is everywhere. It is offered to us all the time and wherever we are. All creatures, friends or foes, pour it out in abundance, and it flows through every fiber of our body and soul until it reaches the very core of our being. If we open our mouths they will be filled. God's activity runs through the universe. It wells up and around and penetrates every created being. Where they are, there it is also. It goes ahead of them, it is with them and it follows them. All they have to do is let its waves sweep them onwards. If only kings and their ministers, princes of the Church and of the world, priests, soldiers and ordinary people knew how easy it would be for them to become very holy! All they need to do is fulfill faithfully the simple duties of Christianity and those called for by their state of life, accept cheerfully all the troubles they meet and submit to God's will in all that they have to do or suffer—without, in any way, seeking out trouble for themselves. It is this attitude which gave such holiness to those patriarchs and prophets who lived long before there were so many methods of spirituality and so many directors of souls. This is the true spirituality, which is valid for all times and for everybody. We cannot become truly good in a better, more marvelous, and yet easier way than by the simple use of the means offered us by God, the unique director of souls. It is the ready acceptance of all that comes to us at each moment of our lives.

(4) *To become perfect we need not understand the designs of God, but only obey them.*

The designs of God—what he chooses to do, his will, his actions, and his grace—are all one and the same thing, all working together to enable us to reach perfection. And perfection is neither more nor less than the soul's faithful co-operation with God. This co-operation begins, grows and comes to fruition in our souls so secretly that we are not aware of it. Theology is crammed with theories and explanations about the wonders of this state. We may know all about these theories and be able to speak and write about them brilliantly, teach them to others and give spiritual advice, but if we have only an intellectual knowledge of them we are compared to those who do God's will and yet know absolutely nothing of theology and certainly cannot talk about its complexities, like a doctor who is ill compared with simple people who enjoy perfect health. If a faithful soul accepts

God's will and purpose in all simplicity, he will reach perfection without ever realizing it, just as a sick man who swallows his medicine obediently will be cured, although he neither knows nor cares about medicine. We need know nothing about the chemistry of combustion to enjoy the warmth of a fire. Holiness is produced in us by the will of God and our acceptance of it. It is not produced by intellectual speculation about it. If we are thirsty we must have a drink and not worry about books which explain what thirst is. If we waste time seeking an explanation about thirst, all that will happen is that we shall get thirstier. It is the same when we thirst after holiness. The desire to know more about it will only drive it further away. We must put all speculation aside and, with childlike willingness, accept all that God presents to us. What God arranges for us to experience at each moment is the best and holiest thing that could happen to us.

(5) *The reading of good books and any other pious exercises are useless unless they are the channels through which God operates.*

All our learning should consist of finding out what God has planned for us at each moment. Anything we read which is not chosen for us by God is harmful. We receive grace through the will of God, and this grace works within us through our reading and through everything else we do. Without God, all our theorizing and reading are useless, and, as they are without the life-giving power of God, all they do is drain the heart and fill the mind. The will of God working in the soul of a simple, ignorant girl through quite ordinary sufferings and actions produces deep within her a supernatural activity yet leaves her quite humble. How different this is from the case of the man, proud of his intellect, who reads spiritual books only out of curiosity and with no link to God. What happens to him? Well, he receives only the dead letter of the message and his heart grows steadily harder and more shrunken.

The designs of God and his will give life to the soul in

whatever guise they appear, nourishing and developing it by giving it what is best for it. This happy state is not brought about by any special happening, but by what God has willed for each moment. What was the best thing for us to do in the moment that has passed is no longer so, for the will of God is now manifesting itself in those circumstances which are the duty of the present moment. It is the fulfilling of this duty, no matter in what guise it presents itself, which does most to make one holy. For example, if it is God's will that the present moment should be spent in reading, then reading will exert a mystical power in the depths of the soul; but if he wishes us to abandon reading for the duty of contemplation, then it is contemplation which will work on our souls and reading would be useless and detrimental; if he wants us to put aside contemplation in order to hear confessions even for a very considerable time, this duty unites us with Jesus Christ, and all the sweetness of contemplation would then only destroy this union.

All our moments are made productive by our obedience to the will of God, which reveals itself in a thousand different ways, each of which successively becomes our immediate duty. Together they mold and perfect within us that "new-self" (Eph. 4:24) until we reach that complete fulfillment of ourselves which God's wisdom has ordained for us. This mysterious growth of Jesus Christ in our souls is the end determined by God, the fruit of his grace and his holy will. As I have said, this fruit is produced, grows and is fed by the stream of duties put before us by God. By discharging these duties, we can be certain we are choosing "the better part" (Luke 10:42). We have to do nothing except allow his holy will to work within us and surrender ourselves to it blindly with absolute confidence. His will is all-wise, all-powerful and infinitely kind to all who trust it completely and without reserve, to all who love it and seek nothing else, believe with firm faith and resolute confidence that what it assigns for each moment is best, and do not go around seeking for other things or try to fathom the links between events and God's designs—which are merely inquiries prompted by self-love. All things owe their nature, their reality and their strength to the will of God, which adapts them so they benefit our souls. Without it, all is nothing, empty and false, vanity, mere husks and death. It is the salvation, the well-being and the life of the body and the soul. We must not scrutinize things to see if they will benefit our mind or body. It is not important. The will of God confers upon all things the power to implant Jesus Christ in the depths of our hearts. We must not attempt to set limits to this omnipotent will.

It does not matter what ideas fill the mind, nor what the body feels, whether the mind is distracted and worried or the body suffering or dying. The will of God is always for the present moment the life of the body and of the soul, for both of them, no matter in what condition they are, are sustained by it alone. Bread is a poison without it; with it, poison is a safe medicine; without it, books only confuse the mind; but with it, confusion becomes clarity. It is all that is good and true in everything and gives us God in all things. He is the all-perfect being, and when we possess him we need nothing else.

(6) *The use of our reason and other faculties is profitable only when it serves as an instrument of God's activity.*

The mind and all its activities would like to hold first place among the tools used by God, but it must be relegated to the lowest, as if it were a dangerous slave, a slave from which a really good man could benefit greatly if he knew how to handle it, but one which could also harm him seriously if it were not kept under tight control. When we crave to be helped by conventional means, God tells us that his action is all we need. When, on the other hand and without good reason, we wish to dispense with external help, God tells us that such help is an instrument which must be neither casually used nor rejected, but employed sincerely and naturally to serve his designs, used with total detachment, as if we had nothing though we have everything.

God's action is boundless in its scope and power, but it can only fill our souls if we empty them of all false confidence in our own ability. This false confidence can check the activity of God within us. God can, when he pleases, change all other obstacles into aids for spiritual progress. For, to him, everything is the same, equally useful or equally useless. Without him everything is nothing, and with him nothing is everything. We may meditate, indulge in contemplation, pray aloud, practice interior silence, live an active life or one withdrawn from the world, and though they may all be valuable, there is nothing better for us than to do what God wants at any particular moment. We must regard everything else with complete indifference and as something worth nothing at all. As we see only God in everything, we must take or leave all things according to his will, so that we neither live, nor develop, nor hope except as he ordains, and never try to use things which have neither power nor worth except through him. We must at all times and in all circumstances say with St. Paul: "Lord, what do you want me to do?" (Acts 9:6). We must not pick and choose. We must say: "I will do everything you wish. My mind wants to do one thing, my body another, but, Lord, I want to do nothing but obey your holy will. Work or every kind of prayer, vocal or mental, active or passive, are all nothing unless your will gives them meaning. All my devotion is to your holy will, not for the things of this world, however grand and noble they are, for grace is given to us because of the love in our hearts and not for any outstanding qualities of our minds."

What makes us holy is the presence of God through the dwelling of the Blessed Trinity in the depths of our hearts when we give them up to God's will. Now, contemplation produces this close union of us with God, as indeed do other acts, provided, of course, that they are part of God's plan for us. Yet contemplation stands supreme, for it is the most effective means of achieving this union, if God wills it.

So we are quite right to love contemplation and all other pious acts, with the clear understanding that this love is really focused on the God of all goodness, who wants us to use every means that will unite us with him. If we entertain a prince, we naturally entertain him and his court. He would be insulted if we neglected his attendants with the excuse that we wanted to honor only him.

(7) *We cannot enjoy true peace unless we submit to God's will.*

If we do not concentrate entirely on doing the will of God we shall find neither happiness nor holiness, no matter what pious practices we adopt, however excellent they may be. If you are not satisfied with what God chooses for you, what else can please you? Does the food prepared for you by God himself disgust you? Well, can you say what other food would not seem stale to someone with so perverted a taste? We must realize that we cannot be really fed, strengthened, purified, enriched and made holy unless we fulfill the duties of the present moment. What else do you want? Why look elsewhere? Are you wiser than God? Why do you seek anything different from what he desires? Do you imagine, considering his wisdom and goodness, that he can be wrong? When you come across something ordained by this wisdom and goodness you must surely be convinced of its excellence. Do you for one moment imagine you will find peace by resisting the Almighty? It is rather this resistance, which we often keep up without realizing it, that is the source of all our trouble. It is only right that if we are discontented with what God offers us every moment, we should be punished by finding nothing else that will content us. If books, the example of the saints and discussions about spiritual matters, do nothing but disturb our peace of mind, and if we feel satiated but unsatisfied by them, it is a sure sign that we have not truly abandoned ourselves to God's will, that we are occupying ourselves with these things out of self-love. They prevent God's entry into our souls, and so we must get rid of these obstacles. Provided, though, that God desires us to have them, we must accept them like everything else as part of God's plan for us. We take them, use them, abandon them as soon as their purpose is over and attend to the work of the present moment. In reality, nothing benefits us that does not arise from God's will, and there is absolutely nothing that gives us more peace or does more to make us holy than obeying the will of God.

(8) *There is only one way to judge how holy we are:
how closely we obey the will of God.*

This will clothes all things with a supernatural, a celestial
significance. His will is supreme. Everything it touches glows
with a divine radiance. In order to keep on the straight road
leading to perfection, we must make quite sure that all
spiritual promptings we receive are from God. We shall know
they are not divinely inspired if they withdraw us from the
duties of our state of life. For these duties are the clearest
indication of God's will, and nothing should supersede them.
There is nothing we need fear in them, nothing we should
ignore, nothing we have to choose. They present no problem.
All the time we spend in fulfilling these duties is most
precious and profitable for us, as we can be sure that we are
obeying God's holy will. Holiness consists in following the
designs of God, and so we must reject nothing, seek nothing,
accept all that comes from him and nothing else. Books, the
advice of the learned, vocal and interior prayer, will all
instruct and guide us toward unity with him, provided he
has willed us them. Quietism is quite wrong when it condemns these means and the use of our senses, for God desires that some people should travel along this road. This is
obvious from their way of life and from their spiritual
indications. It is a waste of time to try to picture any kind of
self-abandonment which excludes all personal activity and
seeks only quiescence, for if God wishes us to act for ourselves, then action makes us holy. For some, God wills only
that they should attend to the duties of their everyday life
and to what other matters he confronts them with. They
need do nothing else to achieve perfection. For others, God
may demand the accomplishment of things which go beyond
their ordinary duties. Those upon whom he makes this demand will recognize it because they will be attracted by it
and will, as it were, feel inspired. If we are one of these, the
best thing we can do is to go where inspiration leads us, without ever neglecting to do what we are commanded to do and
obeying always those commands which God may unex-

pectedly give us. Saints are made by God just as he wishes. They are made according to his plan, and every one of them falls in with this plan. This submission is real self-abandonment, and nothing could be better.

All saints must fulfill the duties imposed on them by their state of life and by God. They live hidden and obscure lives and avoid the dangers of this evil world. They are not saints because of this, but solely because of their submission to the will of God. The more complete their submission, the greater their holiness. Yet we must not make the mistake of thinking that those holy men and women whose virtues shine out because of their wonderful and unusual activities are thereby less completely abandoned to God's designs. If they were content only to practice their ordinary duties once God had demanded these extraordinary activities from them, they would be setting themselves against him by disobeying his will, and no longer would every moment be passed in his service. They have to exert themselves, stretch themselves to their full capacity to meet the demands of God. The inspirations which come to them through grace must be followed. There are, of course, people whose duties are set out for them by the ordinary Christian laws, and they must be limited by these laws, for that is the restriction God imposes upon them; but it must always be remembered that there are others, though they are bound by these laws, who must also obey that other law, that law working on their inmost being, which is imprinted on their hearts by the Holy Spirit.

Who among us is the holiest? To try to find out is pointless. Everyone must follow the appointed path. Holiness consists in obeying God and working with him to the best of our abilities. Making comparisons between various states is meaningless, for holiness is not to be looked for in the number or kind of duties given us. If we act out of self-love or if we do not stamp it out as soon as we are aware of it, we shall stay poor in the midst of a plenty that is not part of God's design. Still, I would like to give some kind of answer to the question, and what I think is this: our holiness is measured by our love of God, and it increases in proportion to the growth of our desire to obey his will and his plans for us, no matter what they are. We can see this in Jesus, Mary and

Joseph. There was more love than grandeur in their personal lives, more spirituality than formality. There is nothing to tell us that they sought holiness in things and events, but only in the way they dealt with them. So we must recognize that there is no special or singular road leading to perfection but that for most people easily the best thing is submission to all that God wills for their particular way of life.

(9)   *To become holy is very easy when this doctrine is properly understood.*

I believe that people trying to be holy would be saved a lot of trouble if they were taught to follow the right path, and I am writing of people who lived ordinary lives in the world and of those specially marked by God. Let the former realize what lies hidden in every moment of the day and the duties each one brings, and let the latter appreciate the fact that things they regard as trivial and of no importance are essential to sanctity. And let them both be aware that holiness means the eager acceptance of every trial sent them by God. This is vastly superior to the enjoyment of all extraordinary experiences. It is the philosophers' stone which changes into gold all their worries, all their troubles, all their sufferings. Let them realize this—and then how happy they will be! Let them realize that all they have to do to achieve the height of holiness is to do only what they are already doing and endure what they are already enduring, and to realize, too, that all they count as trivial and worthless is what can make them holy. How I would like to preach the virtues of your holy will and teach everyone that nothing is easier, more ordinary and more within reach than holiness! The good and the bad thieves had nothing different to do and suffer to become saints. So let us take two ordinary people. One is wholly worldly, the other spiritual, yet the demands made upon them are equal. Yet the one achieves eternal happiness because he submits gladly to your holy will, but the other damns himself because, given the same tasks, he undertakes them with a sullen reluctance. Their hearts are very different.

Now, you who read this—and you are very dear to me— must realize that I am asking nothing extraordinary from you. All I want is for you to carry on as you are doing and endure what you have to do—but change your attitude to all these things. And this change is simply to say "I will" to all that God asks. What is easier? For who could refuse obedience to a will so kind and so good? By this obedience we shall become one with God.

CHAPTER II

EMBRACE THE PRESENT MOMENT AS AN EVER-FLOWING SOURCE OF HOLINESS

(1) *The activity of God is everywhere and always present, but it is visible only to the eye of faith.*

All creatures live in the hands of God. By our senses we can see only the action of the creature, but faith sees the creator acting in all things. Faith sees that Jesus Christ lives in everything and works through all history to the end of time, that every fraction of a second, every atom of matter, contains a fragment of his hidden life and his secret activity. The actions of created beings are veils which hide the profound mysteries of the workings of God. After the Resurrection, Jesus Christ took the disciples unawares by his appearances, showing himself to them as if disguised and then appearing when he had revealed himself. And it is this same Jesus, ever living and ever active, who still surprises us if our faith is not strong and clear-sighted enough. There is never a moment when God does not come forward in the guise of some suffering or some duty, and all that takes place within us, around us and through us both includes and hides his activity. Yet, because it is invisible, we are always taken by surprise and do not recognize his operation until it has passed by us. If we could lift the veil and if we watched with vigilant attention, God would endlessly reveal himself to us and we should see and rejoice in his active presence in all that befalls us. At every event we should exclaim: "It is the Lord!" (John 21:7). Nothing could happen to us without our accepting it as a gift from God. We should regard all creatures as very feeble tools serving his purpose; we should realize, too, that we are in want of nothing and that his continual care for us makes him give us everything that is good and proper. If we had faith, we should be grateful to all creatures, cherish them and thank them silently for their good will in helping us, by God's design, toward perfection.

If we never ceased to live the life of faith, our intercourse with God would never be interrupted and we should talk with him face to face. When we speak it is the air which transmits our thoughts and our words, and so all our actions and our sufferings would be the medium through which we heard the expression of God's will. They would, as it were, give his Word substance and visible expression, and all that happened to us would be seen as holy and most excellent. God in his glory will give us this union in heaven; here on earth we can enjoy it by faith. The only difference is the way it is given to us.

It is faith which interprets God for us. Without its light we should not even know that God was speaking, but would hear only the confused, meaningless babble of creatures. As Moses saw the flame of fire in the bush and heard the voice of God coming from it, so faith will enable us to understand his hidden signs, so that amidst all the apparent clutter and disorder we shall see all the loveliness and perfection of divine wisdom. Faith transforms the earth into paradise. By it our hearts are raised with the joy of our nearness to heaven. Every moment reveals God to us. Faith is our light in this life. By it we know the truth without seeing it, we are put in touch with what we cannot feel, recognize what we cannot see, and view the world stripped of all its superficialities. Faith unlocks God's treasury. It is the key to all the vastness of his wisdom. The hollowness of all created things is disclosed by faith, and it is by faith that God makes his presence plain everywhere. Faith tears aside the veil so that we can see the everlasting truth.

All that lies around us is false and vain. There is no truth except in God, and there is an immeasurable distance between his thoughts and our illusions. It is incredible that, although we have been warned time and time again that all the affairs of the world are but shadows and mysteries to be understood only by faith, we still persist in looking at them as if they had an intrinsic value and reality. The result is that everything remains a riddle to us. We behave like fools. What we should do is gaze at the principle, the source and the origin of all things. Then we should find that everything has a supernatural quality, something divine about it that can lead us onward to holiness. Everything is part of that completeness which is Jesus Christ, and all that happens, every event, is a stone toward the building of that heavenly Jerusalem where one day we may dwell. If we persist in living according to what we see and feel, we shall wander like imbeciles through a maze shrouded with darkness and phantasmagoria. Yet, by faith, we should know God and be able to live for him alone, ignoring all the frivolities of external things.

(2) *The will of God often appears repulsive, but faith enables us to see it as it really is.*

If we live by faith we shall judge things very differently from the way people do who rely only on the evidence of their senses and so remain unaware of the priceless treasure hidden under appearances. If we know that someone in disguise is really our king we shall behave very differently toward him than will someone who sees only an ordinary man. He will treat him as such. Now, if we see the will of God in the most trifling affairs, in every misfortune, and in every disaster, we shall accept them all with an equal joy, delight and respect. What others fear and flee from, we shall welcome with open doors. The clothing is shabby and mean to the ordinary eye, but we shall respect the royal majesty hidden under it and feel a deepening of our love the more hidden and abject our king is. I cannot describe what the heart feels when it accepts the divine will so apparently diminished in power, so humble and so pitiful. How profoundly moved Mary's loving heart was when she saw the poverty of her God, lying whimpering and trembling on a bundle of hay in a manger! If we could ask the people of Bethlehem what they thought of this child, we know what answer we should get. Yet, had he been born in a palace surrounded with all the trappings of a prince, they would have rushed to pay him honor. But let us ask Mary, Joseph, the Magi and the shepherds, and they will tell us that in this utter poverty they find something indescribable which increases the glory of God and his attractiveness. Paradoxically, what we cannot experience by our senses stimulates, increases and enriches our faith. The less we see, the more we believe.

To adore Jesus on Thabor, or to accept the will of God expressed through remarkable circumstances, does not prove that our faith is stronger or better than to accept gladly God's will in the petty affairs of life and to worship Jesus nailed to the cross, for our faith is never more alive than when what we experience through our senses contradicts and tries to destroy it. The battle with our senses gives our faith a splendid victory. To discover God just as clearly in very minor or ordinary things as in the big things of life, is to have a far from normal faith. It is one that is great and extraordinary.

To be satisfied with the present moment is to relish and adore the divine will moving through all we have to do and suffer as events crowd in upon us. If we are like this, the liveliness of our faith will compel us to adore God no matter how humiliating the circumstances in which he places us. There is nothing which can conceal him from the penetrating gaze of our faith. If our senses insist, "There is no God," the more closely and firmly do we clasp to us our bunch of myrrh. We are neither astonished nor disgusted by anything.

Mary sees the Apostles flee, but she herself remains faithfully at the foot of the cross. Torn by wounds and disfigured with spittle though he was, she knew him as her son. Indeed, his bleeding, battered body increased her love and adoration of him. The more viciously he was blasphemed, the more she venerated him. The life of faith is the untiring pursuit of God through all that disguises and disfigures him and, as it were, destroys and annihilates him. Look at Mary: from the stable to Calvary she stayed close to that God who was despised, rejected and persecuted. So it is with all faithful souls. They have to pass through a steady succession of veils and shadows and illusions which seek to hide the will of God, but they follow and love it even to the death on the cross. They know that they must leave the shadows and run after this divine sun which, from its rising to its setting and no matter how thick and dark the clouds hiding it, illumines, warms and sets aglow the loyal hearts who bless, praise and contemplate it as it sweeps along its mysterious course. Let us, then, as faithful souls, happy and tireless, advance after the beloved as he moves with giant strides across the heavens. He sees all things. He walks above the smallest blades of grass and the cedar groves, and treads the grains of sand as well as the mountain peaks. Wherever we have trodden he has been, and if we constantly pursue him we shall find him no matter where we are.

There is no peace more wonderful than the peace we enjoy when faith shows us God in all created things. All that is dark becomes light, and what is bitter sweet. Faith transforms ugliness into beauty, and malice into kindness. Faith is the mother of tenderness, trust and joy. It cannot feel anything but love and pity for its enemies, by whom it is so greatly enriched, for the more harsh the actions of creatures against us, the more beneficial God makes them for our souls. The human instrument tries to injure us, but the divine craftsman, in whose hands it is, ensures that it takes from our souls all that would harm them. The will of God has only delights, favors and riches for all souls who are obedient to it. We cannot trust it too much or abandon ourselves to it too completely. If we leave everything to God, he will do all that is necessary for our holiness. Faith cannot doubt this. The more unreliable, disgusted, despairing and unsure of themselves our senses are, the more emphatically does faith exclaim: "God is here! All goes well!" There is nothing that faith cannot overcome. It pierces through the darkest shadows and the thickest clouds to reach the truth, embraces it and can never be torn from it.

(3) *Every moment is crammed with infinite riches which are given us according to the extent of our faith and love.*

Once we can grasp that each moment contains some sign of the will of God, we shall find in it all we can possibly desire, for there is nothing more reasonable, more excellent, more holy than his will. Can any variations of time, place or circumstance add anything to its infinite value? If you are taught the secret of finding its presence in every moment of your lives, then you possess all that is most precious and supremely worthwhile. What is it that you want—those of you seeking perfection? Give your desires free reign, setting absolutely no limits, no boundaries to them. Listen to me: let your hearts demand the infinite, for I can tell you how to fill them. There is never one moment in which I cannot show you how to find whatever you can desire. The present moment is always overflowing with immeasurable riches, far more than you are able to hold. Your faith will measure it out to you: as you believe, so you will receive. Love, too, is also a measure. The more you love the more you will want and the more you will get. Every moment the will of God is stretched out before us like a vast ocean which the desires of our hearts can never empty, but more and more of it will be ours as our souls grow in faith, in trust and in love. The entire universe cannot fill and satisfy our hearts, for they are greater than all apart from God. Mountains which overawe us are but tiny grains to our hearts. We must draw upon that will veiled and hidden beneath every little detail of our lives and shall find there a fullness, an amplitude infinitely more vast than all our longings. Fawn upon no one and have no illusions. They can do nothing for us. The will of God alone can satisfy us. That is what we must adore and drive direct toward it, casting aside all superficialities. Strip away the fascination of the senses, kill and destroy them, and then you will be ruled by faith, for your senses worship created things. Take away from the senses what they worship and they will weep like deserted children, but faith must triumph, for nothing can destroy the will of God. When the senses are really attacked, starved and stripped they collapse, and faith becomes stronger and more alive than ever. This faith laughs at the importance of the senses, as the commander of an impregnable citadel laughs at all attacks launched against it. When the will of God has been made known to us and we, in turn, make it plain that we are only too glad to abandon ourselves to it, we shall be given most powerful help. We shall then know the joy of God's arrival within us and savor it more intensely the more completely we abandon ourselves to his adorable will.

(4) God *reveals himself to us through the most common-place happenings in a way just as mysterious and just as truly and as worthy of adoration as in the great occurrences of history and the Scriptures.*

The written word of God is full of mysteries, and equally so is his word expressed in world events. These two books are truly sealed, and it can be said of both of them: "The letters bring death" (II Cor. 3:6). God is the center of faith, and faith is a gulf of shadows, and these shadows emerge and veil all the divine operations. All his words and all his works are only, as it were, murky rays from a clouded sun. With our bodily eyes we can see the natural sun and its beams, but the eyes of our soul, by which we want to see God and his works, remain shut. There is darkness instead of light; knowledge is ignorance and we see without understanding. Holy Scripture is the mysterious utterance of a still more mysterious God, and the events of history are the incomprehensible words of this same hidden and unknown God. They are dark drops from an ocean of darkness and shadows. Every drop of water and every little stream carry traces of their source. The fall of the angels and of Adam, the ungodliness and idolatry of men up to and after the flood in the lifetime of the patriarchs, who knew and told their children the story of the creation and of the still recent preservation of the world from the flood—these are indeed some of the most mysterious accounts in Holy Scripture. Then we have a mere handful of men kept safe from idolatry until the coming of the Messiah, in spite of the general loss of faith throughout the world, with iniquity always dominant, always powerful, and the little band of believers always ill-used and perse-cuted. Think of the treatment of Jesus Christ. And the plagues of the Apocalypse. Imagine it! These are God's words.

It is what he has revealed. The consequences of these terrible mysteries will continue to the end of time, and yet they are still the living word, teaching us of the wisdom, the power and the goodness of God. These divine attributes are made manifest by all the events of history. All things teach this truth. But, alas, we cannot see it, though we must believe it is so.

Why does God allow Turks and heretics to flourish? They proclaim his infinite perfection. That is the sole purpose of Pharaoh and all the impious men who have followed his example. It is no use looking at these historical facts and figures in the ordinary way. We must shut our eyes and cease to reason if we wish to see the divine mysteries in these affairs.

You speak, Lord, to all men in general by the great events of history. All revolutions are only the waves of your providence raising storms and tempests in the minds of those who question your mysterious actions. You speak to every individual through what happens to them moment by moment. Instead of hearing the voice of God in all these things and revering the mysterious obscurity of his word, however, men see in them only material happenings, the effects of chance or purely human activities. They find fault with everything, want to change this continual expression of God's word and give themselves absolute freedom to commit every kind of excess, the very least of which they would consider a monstrous outrage if it involved a single comma in Holy Scripture. "That is the word of God," they say, "and all that is there is holy and true." The less they understand it, the more they venerate it and adore the depths of God's wisdom. Very right and proper, too. But when God speaks to us at every moment, not with words of ink on paper but by what we suffer and do from moment to moment, should we not give equal attention to him? Why do we not venerate his truth and goodness in all this? But we are pleased by nothing and critical of everything. For we are judging by our senses and our reason that which can only be measured by faith. We read, with the eyes of faith, the word of God in the Scriptures, and we are very wrong to read it with other eyes when it comes to us in his activities.

(5) *God continues to write his word in our hearts, but the characters will not be seen until the day of judgment.*

"Jesus Christ is the same today as he was yesterday and as he will be forever," says the Apostle Paul (Heb. 13:8).

From the creation of the world, Jesus Christ has lived in every human soul and he works within us throughout our lives. All the years from the beginning of the world until its end are but as a day. Jesus lived before its creation and he lives still. He began in himself and continues in his saints a life that will never end. O life of Jesus which embraces and transcends all eras! A life which generates fresh activities every moment! If the whole world could not hold all that Jesus said and did (John 21:25) and all the workings of his interior life, if the Gospels give only a slight sketch of a few little details, if the first hour of his earthly life is so little known and yet so fruitful, how many gospels would need to be written to tell the detailed story of that mystical life of Jesus Christ which spreads and develops marvels without end?—for, strictly speaking, the whole of history is nothing but the story of God's activity.

With absolute truth, the Holy Spirit has recorded a few of the moments in this vast stretch of time. In the Scriptures he has collected a few drops from this ocean of time and enabled us to see the hidden and unknown ways by which he brought about the appearance of Jesus Christ in the world. Amidst all the confusion among the tribes of humanity, we can trace the origin, the race and the family tree of this first-born child. The whole of the Old Testament is only a small diagram showing innumerable and mysterious tracks, and contains nothing but what is necessary to lead us to Jesus. The Holy Spirit has kept everything else hidden among the richness of his wisdom. From all the vast ocean of his activity, he allows only a trickle of water to escape which, after reaching Jesus, is lost in the Apostles and engulfed in the Apocalypse. Thus the rest of the story of the activity of Jesus in the souls of good people until the end of time can be known only by faith. We are now living in a time of faith. The Holy Spirit writes no more gospels except in our hearts. All we do from moment to moment is live this new gospel of the Holy Spirit. We, if we are holy, are the paper; our sufferings and our actions are the ink. The workings of the Holy Spirit are his pen, and with it he writes a living gospel; but it will never be read until that last day of glory when it leaves the printing press of this life.

And what a splendid book it will be—the book the Holy Spirit is still writing! The book is on press and never a day passes when type is not set, ink applied and pages pulled. But we remain in the light of faith. The paper is blacker than the ink and the type is pied; the language is not of this world and we understand nothing. We shall be able to read it only in heaven. We could understand something of the complexity of God's activity if we could see our fellow humans not just as they appear superficially but in their very essence and see, too, how God is working on and within them. Yet there are difficulties. How can we read this book when its letters are unknown, of infinite variety and upside down, and its pages smeared with ink? Just think what an infinite number of different and worthwhile books are produced by the mixing up of twenty-six letters. We cannot understand this wonder, so how can we comprehend what God is doing in the universe? How can we read and understand so vast a book, one in which every single letter has its own special meaning and, within its tiny shape, contains the most profound mysteries? We can neither see nor feel these mysteries. Only by faith can they be known.

And it is by their origin that faith judges how true and good they are, for in themselves these mysteries are so obscure that our mere reason can understand nothing of them.

So teach me, Holy Spirit, to read in this book of life! I long to become your disciple and, like a little child, to believe in what I cannot see. It is enough for me that my master speaks. He talks and explains, arranges the letters of the book and makes it comprehensible. That is all I need. I am convinced that everything is just as he says, although I cannot see why.

But I know he is truth itself and he says nothing but the truth. He puts letters together to make a word, assembles more to form another. There are perhaps only three or six. But they are exactly right. Any different number would make nonsense. After all, he alone knows the thoughts of men, and so he alone can put them into words. Everything is significant and everything makes perfect sense. A line ends because he wants it to. There is not a single comma missing, or one full stop too many. Although I believe now, when the day of glory dawns the secrets of so many mysteries will be shown to me that I shall realize how imperfect my knowledge was during my earthly life. What now seems to me so confused, so incoherent, so foolish and so fanciful will then delight and entrance me by its order, its beauty, its wisdom and the incomprehensible wonders I shall explore for all eternity.

(6)   *The work of God in its daily manifestations is often treated by many Christians as Jesus Christ was treated by the Jews.*

There is so much unbelief in the world, for too many people speak of God unworthily and never stop finding fault with his activities in a manner they would not dare use toward the most incompetent workman. What we really want to do is restrict his work so that it conforms to the rules and boundaries that our limited reason considers suitable. We try to improve and do nothing but complain and grumble. Yet we are surprised at the way the Jews treated Jesus Christ! Ah! when I think of God's love, his adorable will, his unerring acts, I cannot believe how he is treated. How can the will of God be unreasonable? How can it ever be wrong? Yet we say: "There's this bit of business of mine. I need this. What I want has been taken from me. My neighbor is hindering the good works I want to do. Now, isn't this quite unreasonable? And, on top of it all, I fall ill just when I should be fit."

Now let me tell you that the will of God is all that is necessary, and what it does not give you is of no use to you at all. My friends, you lack nothing. You would be very ashamed if you knew what the experiences you call setbacks, upheavals, pointless disturbances, and tedious annoyances really are. You would realize that your complaints about them are nothing more nor less than blasphemies—though that never occurs to you. Nothing happens to you except by the will of God, and yet his beloved children curse it because they do not know it for what it is.

When you lived on earth, Jesus, the Jews regarded you as possessed by a devil and as a Samaritan (John 8:48). Now, today, how do we regard that adorable will of yours? What do we think of you, you who live as the centuries drift past, always worthy of all praise and honor? Has there ever been a single moment, from the creation of the world until now, or until the end of time, when the holy name of God has not merited all praise? It is a name which resounds through every age and through all that happens in every moment of all those ages. It makes all things holy. Can we imagine that the will of God will hurt us? Should I be afraid of, or flee, from his name? Where could I find anything better if I am afraid of God's action on me? After all, it is the work of his divine will.

Now how should we listen to God, who speaks to us in the depths of our hearts at every moment of our lives? We have our normal senses and our intelligence, but what if they cannot understand the truth and goodness of his words? Is it because they are too feeble to cope with the divine truths? But should we really be astonished that our human reason is baffled by the divine mysteries? When God speaks he uses mysterious words, and they are a death blow to all that we are as rational human beings, for all the mysteries of God destroy our physical senses and our intellectuality. These mysteries revitalize the heart, but they bewilder the rest of us. By the same stroke God kills and gives life, but the keener the pains of death, the more intensely does life flow into the soul. The darker the mystery, the more we are illumined by it. So a simple soul finds God where he seems not to appear at all. If we want to live a life of faith we must fight without pause against our senses.

(7)   *The love of God comes to us through all creatures but hidden as it is in the Blessed Sacrament.*

How many and great are the truths hidden from us! And how true it is that every painful trial, all we have to do and every impulse of the spirit, give us God exactly as he comes to us in the mystery of the Blessed Sacrament. Nothing is more certain. For both reason and faith tell us that God's love is present in every creature and in every event, just as Jesus Christ and the Church inform us that the sacred body and blood of God are truly present in the Eucharist. His love wishes to unite itself with us through all that the world contains, all that he had created, ordained and allowed. That is his supreme purpose, and to accomplish it he uses both the best and worst of his creatures, the most unpleasant and the most delightful of happenings. The more naturally repugnant to us the chosen means, the more meritorious is our acceptance of them. So every moment of our lives can be a kind of communion with his love, a communion which can produce in our souls fruits similar to those we receive with the body and blood of the Son of God. This latter has, it is true, a sacramental power which the former cannot have; but yet how much oftener can we experience the former and its merit will continually increase as our dispositions develop toward perfection. The most holy of lives is a mysterious thing because of its very simplicity and apparently humble state. What a festival and never-ending feast is ours! God ceaselessly gives himself and is received with no pomp and circumstance, but hidden beneath all that is weak and foolish and worthless. He chooses what our natural feelings despise and what our human prudence rejects. From these castoffs he creates miracles of love and gives himself to us as often as we believe we have found him there.

(8) *The disclosure that each moment brings is of such great value because it is meant for us personally.*

We are really well taught only by the words which God addresses especially to us. Neither books nor laborious delving into history will instruct us about the wisdom of God. They will fill us with a useless, muddled kind of knowledge and puff us up with pride. It is what happens moment by moment which enlightens us and gives us that practical knowledge which Jesus Christ himself chose to acquire before beginning his public life. The Gospel tells us how he "increased in wisdom" (Luke 2:52), although, as God, all wisdom was already his. This knowledge that comes to us only through experience is absolutely necessary if we want to touch the hearts of those God sends to us. We can understand nothing perfectly except what experience has taught through what we have suffered and done. Our master is the Holy Spirit, who gives us these words of life, and all we say to others must come from him. All we read and study becomes fruitful, clear and effective under the guidance of experience. Without it, we are dough without yeast or salt. Our ideas are vague and ill-directed. We are like absent-minded people who know all about geography but lose their way when going home. So we must listen to God moment by moment to become learned in this practical theology of virtue. Take no notice of what is said to other people. Listen only to what is said to and for you. There will be enough there to strengthen your faith, for it will be exercised, purified and deepened by the very obscurity of these communications.

(9) *The present moment is an ever-flowing source of holiness.*

Are we thirsty? Then we have not far to go to find the fountain of living water. It bubbles up near us at every moment. How foolish it is to tire ourselves by searching for tiny rivulets which can never quench our thirst. Only the fountain can satisfy us. It is inexhaustible. Do you want to think, write and live like prophets, apostles and saints? Then you must surrender, as they did, to the inspirations of God.

O unknown Love! It would seem that all your wonders are over and done with and that there is nothing left to do but copy your old works and repeat your utterances of the past. We do not see that your activity can ever be exhausted and that it is an endless source of fresh thoughts, new sufferings, new deeds, a source of new patriarchs, prophets, apostles and saints who have no need to copy anything written and done before their time but simply spend their lives in continual abandonment of themselves to your hidden guidance. We are always hearing of "the early centuries" and "the days of the saints." What a way to speak! Surely we must realize that in every age, including this one, God's will works through every moment, making each one holy and giving it a supernatural quality. Can we imagine that in the days of old there was a secret method of abandoning oneself to the divine will that is now out of date? And had the saints of those early times any other secret apart from that of obeying God's will from moment to moment? And will not God continue until the end of the world to pour out his grace upon all the souls who utterly abandon themselves to him?

O adorable Love, eternal, ever fruitful and ever marvelous! You give me all the knowledge and learning I need. You embrace all I think, say, do and suffer. I shall not become what you want me to be by studying your earlier works, but only by welcoming you in all things. By following that old, royal road of our fathers, I shall be enlightened and shall think and speak as they did. That is the way I want to imitate, quote and copy all of them.

(10) *The present moment always reveals the presence and the power of God.*

Every moment we live through is like an ambassador who declares the will of God, and our hearts always utter their acceptance. Our souls steadily advance, never halting, but sweeping along with every wind. Every current, every tech-

nique thrusts us onward in our voyage to the infinite. Everything works to this end and, without exception, helps us toward holiness. We can find all that is necessary in the present
moment. We need not worry about whether to pray or be
silent, whether to withdraw into retreat or mix with people,
to read or write, to meditate or make our minds a receptive
blank, to shun or seek out books on spirituality. Nor do poverty or riches, sickness or health, life or death matter in the
least. What does matter is what each moment produces by
the will of God. We must strip ourselves naked, renounce all
desire for created things, and retain nothing of ourselves or
for ourselves, so that we can be wholly submissive to God's
will and so delight him. Our only satisfaction must be to live
in the present moment as if there were nothing to expect
beyond it.

If what happens to a soul abandoned to God is all that is
necessary for it, it is clear that it can lack nothing and that
it should never complain, for this would show that it lacked
faith and was living by the light of its reason and the evidence of its senses. Neither reason nor the senses are ever
satisfied, for they never see the sufficiency of grace. To hallow
the name of God is, according to the Scriptures, to recognize
his holiness and to love and adore it in all the things which
proceed like words from the mouth of God. For what God
creates at each moment is a divine thought which is expressed
by a thing, and so all these things are so many names and
words through which he makes known his wishes. God's will
is single and individual, with an unknown and inexpressible
name, but it is infinitely diverse in its effects, which are, as
it were, as many as the names it assumes. To hallow God's
name is to know, to worship and to love the ineffable being
who bears it. It is also to know, to worship and to love his
adorable will every moment and all that it does, regarding all
that happens as so many veils, shadows and names beneath
which this eternal and most holy will is always active. It is
holy in all it does, holy in all it says, holy in every manifestation, and holy in all the names it bears.

It is thus that Job blessed the name of God. This holy
man blessed the utter desolation which fell upon him, for it
displayed the will of God. His ruin he regarded as one of

God's names, and in blessing it he was declaring that, no matter how terrible its manifestations, it was always holy under whatever name or form it appeared. And David never ceased to bless it. It is by this continual recognition of the will of God, as displayed and revealed in all things, that God reigns in us, that his will is done on earth as in heaven, and that he nourishes us continually.

The full and complete meaning of self-abandonment to his will is embraced in the matchless prayer given to us by Jesus Christ. By the command of God and the Church we recite it several times a day; but, apart from this, if we love to suffer and obey his adorable will, we shall utter it constantly in the depths of our hearts. When we can utter only through our mouths—which takes time—our hearts can speak instantly, and it is in this manner that simple souls are called to bless God from the depths of their souls. Yet they complain bitterly that they cannot praise him as much as they desire, for God gives to them so much that they feel they cannot cope with such riches. A secret working of the divine wisdom is to pour treasure into the heart whilst impoverishing the senses, so that the one overflows whilst the other is drained and emptied.

The events of every moment are stamped with the will of God. How holy is his name! How right it is to bless it and to treat it as something which sanctifies all it touches. Can we see anything which carries this name without showing it with infinite love? It is a divine warmth from heaven and gives us a ceaseless increase of grace. It is the kingdom of heaven which penetrates the soul. It is the bread of angels which is eaten on earth as well as in heaven. There is nothing trivial about our passing moments, as they enclose the whole kingdom of holiness and the food on which angels feed.

Yes, O Lord, may you rule my heart, nourish it, purify it, make it holy, and let it triumph over all its enemies. Most precious moment! How small it is to my bodily eyes, but how great to the eyes of my faith! How can I think of it as nothing when it is thought of so highly by my heavenly father? All that comes from him is most excellent and bears the imprint of its origin.

(11) *The action of God inspires souls to seek the highest degree of holiness. What is required from each soul is complete abandonment to this activity.*

Because they do not know how to make use of God's action, many people have recourse to too many means to try to reach holiness. All these could be useful if they were ordained by God, but they are harmful when they hinder the simple, straightforward union of the soul with God. Jesus is our master to whom we do not pay enough attention. He speaks to every heart and utters the word of life, the essential word for each one of us, but we do not hear it. We would like to know what he has said to other people, yet we do not listen to what he says to us. We do not try enough to look at things as having been given a supernatural character by God's action. We should always receive them with the confidence they deserve, generously and with an open heart, for none of them can harm us if we welcome them in this manner. This tremendous activity of God, which never varies from the beginning to the end of time, pours itself through every moment and gives itself in all its vastness and power to every clear-hearted soul which adores and loves it and abandons itself without reserve to it.

You say you would be delighted to be able to die for God. You would find great pleasure in such a violent deed or a life that ended up that way. You long to lose everything, to die abandoned by everybody and to sacrifice your life for others. But as for me, Lord, I give all glory to your will. Obedience to it gives me all the joy of martyrdom, austerity and loving my neighbor. Your will is all-sufficient for me, and I am happy to live and die as it ordains. I delight in it for itself alone, quite apart from all it does, pervading all things and rendering all it touches divine. Because of it, all my life seems lived in heaven, my every moment is part of your activity, and, living or dead, I can know no greater bliss. I shall no longer count the times and the manner of your approach, my beloved. You will always be welcome. It seems to me, dear will of God, that you have revealed to me your greatness and there is now no longer anything I can do outside its embrace, which is the same yesterday, tomorrow and forever. From you, O Lord, pours the unending stream of grace. You ensure that it never fails and that it works unceasingly. So I shall no longer try to find you within the narrow limits of a book, in the life of a saint, or in some high-flown philosophy. All these are only drops of that ocean which flows over us all. God's activity moves through everything, and all else are but mere fragments which disappear within it. I shall no longer try to find God's will in spiritual writings. I shall no longer go begging, as it were, from door to door for food for my soul, nor shall I seek anything at all from any created being or thing. Dear Lord, I mean to live so that I may honor you as the son of a father who is infinitely wise, good and powerful. I intend to live according to my beliefs; and, as your will governs all things at all times and is always for my benefit, I will live on this vast income, which can never fail, is always present and always available to do me the greatest possible good. Is there any creature whose works can equal those performed by God? Since his uncreated hands do everything for me, why should I run about seeking help from ignorant, helpless creatures who have no real affection for me? I should die of thirst if I rushed from fountain to fountain, from stream to stream when by my side is an immeasurable stretch of water poured out by your hand. Where else do I need to look? You give me bread to feed me, soap to cleanse me, fire to purify me, and a chisel to shape my human form into one worthy of heaven. You give me everything I need. What I seek elsewhere seeks me out and offers itself to me through all creation.

O Love, why should you be so unknown and why should you, as it were, throw yourself and all your delights at everyone whilst people are trying to find you in hidden corners and obscure places where they will never come across you? How foolish they are not to breathe the fresh air, not to wander about the countryside, not to drink the abundant water, not to recognize and seize hold of God and see his holiness in all things.

My dear souls, you are seeking for secret ways of belonging to God, but there is only one: making use of whatever he offers you. Everything leads you to this union with him. Everything guides you to perfection except what is sinful or not a duty. Accept everything and let him act. All things conduct you and support you. Your way is lined with banners as you advance along it in your carriage. All is in the hand of God. His action is vaster and more pervasive than all the elements of earth, air and water. It enters you through every one of your senses so long as you use them only as he directs, for you must never employ them against his will. God's action penetrates every atom of your body, into the very marrow of your bones. The blood flowing through your veins moves only by his will. The state of your health, whether you are weak or strong, lively or languid, your life and death, all spring from his will, and all your bodily conditions are the workings of grace. Every feeling and every thought you have, no matter how they arise, all come from God's invisible hand. There is no created being who can tell you what his action will achieve within you, but continuing experience will teach you. Uninterruptedly your life will flow through this unfathomed abyss where you have nothing to do but love and cherish what each moment brings, considering it as the best possible thing for you and having perfect confidence in God's activities, which cannot do anything but good.

Yes, divine Love, if all souls would only be satisfied with you, what supernatural, sublime, wonderful and inconceivable heights they would scale! Yes, if only we had sense enough to leave everything to the guidance of God's hand, we should reach the highest peak of holiness. Everyone could do it, for the opportunity is offered to everyone. We have, as it were, only to open our mouths and let holiness flow in. In you every soul has a unique model of surpassing holiness and, by your never-wearying activity, may be made to resemble you. If every soul lived, acted and spoke under the guidance of God, they would have no need to imitate anyone else. Each one of them would be a unique and holy being, made so by the most ordinary means.

How, my Lord, can I make people value what I offer them? I possess so great a treasure that I could shower wealth on everyone, and yet I see souls withering like plants in an arid waste.

You simple souls, who are quite without any piety, have no talents, are quite uneducated, understand nothing of the language of spirituality, and are filled with astonished wonder at the eloquence of the learned—come and I will teach you a secret that will put you far ahead of these clever folk. I will make you so well placed for achieving perfection that you will always find yourself in the midst of it. I will unite you to God and you shall go hand in hand with him from the first moment you begin to do what I shall tell you. Come, I say, come, not to study the map of the realms of the spirit, but to possess it so that you can walk freely about it and never be afraid of getting lost. Come, not to study the record of God's grace, not to learn what it has done down all the centuries and is still doing, but come and be the trusting subject of its operation. There is no need for you to understand the lessons it has taught others, nor to repeat them cleverly. You will be taught matters which are for you alone.

(12)   *Only God's activity can make us holy, for it alone can make us imitate the perfection of our Lord.*

The concept of every single thing in the entire universe has been with the eternal wisdom for all time. As the ages pass, God allows these concepts and ideas to emerge. Now suppose you knew all the concepts which have nothing to do with you, that knowledge could not help you in any way. But God knows the one idea, the one concept according to which you have to develop. He knows all that is needful for the sanctification of every individual soul. Holy Scripture contains one part, and the workings of the Holy Spirit within the soul do the rest, using the particular ideal reserved for you. Now it is surely obvious that the only way to receive the impress of this idea is to put oneself quietly in the hands of God, and that none of our own efforts and mental striving can be of any use at all. This work in our souls cannot be accomplished by cleverness, intelligence, or any subtlety of mind, but only by completely abandoning ourselves to the divine action, becoming like metal poured into a mold, or a canvas waiting for the brush, or marble under the sculptor's hands. It is surely clear that we shall not assume that image which the eternal wisdom wishes us to have by trying to understand all the mysterious activities of God down through the centuries. We can receive God's seal on our souls only by abandoning our will to him, not by any efforts of our reason. The common sense of ordinary souls is simply this: being perfectly satisfied with what it knows is suitable for it, and never attempting to tread beyond the boundaries laid out for it. It is not inquisitive about the way God acts. It is quite happy to submit to his will and makes no attempt to find out its intentions. It wants to know only what every moment says to it, listens to what God utters in the depths of its heart and does not ask what has been said to others. It is fully satisfied with what itself receives, and so, quite unconsciously, it grows constantly nearer to God. God speaks to the soul by what his action produces, and the soul, being quite unaware of this, accepts everything simply and naturally. Such a soul's spirituality is one that is unshakable and floods its entire being. It is not moved by a torrent of confused words and ideas which by themselves would only fill it with pride. People often rely on their intellect in their efforts to become holy, but it is not necessary. It may even hinder them. We must use only what God gives us to do and suffer. What we should not do is neglect the divine reality in our own lives and busy ourselves with the wonders done by God in the past. We should rather try to add to these wonders by our own fidelity.

The marvels of God's activity which delight us when we read about them only serve to make us bored with the small happenings around us. Yet it is these trivialities, as we consider them, which would do marvels for us if only we did not despise them. We are so stupid! We are astonished by and glorify God's activities when we read about them, yet when he wishes to continue writing about them on our hearts we become restive and prevent him from doing so by our curiosity to see what he is doing in and around us. Forgive me, divine Love, for I am setting down here those faults which are mine, and I cannot yet understand how to let you act freely on me. I have not yet myself been cast in the mold designed for me. I have visited all your studios and admired all your creations, but I have not yet become abandoned enough to accept the strokes of your brush. Yet I have found in you a beloved master, a teacher, a father and a most dear friend. I will be your disciple and go to no other school than yours. Like the prodigal son, I will come home hungry for your bread. I will abandon all ideas and books about spiritual matters and have nothing to do with them unless they work together with your will. All I want to do is love you and devote myself to the duties of each moment, and so allow you to act on me as you wish.

CHAPTER III

TO SURRENDER TO GOD IS TO
PRACTICE EVERY VIRTUE

(1) *The life of God in the soul.*

Sometimes we live in God and sometimes God lives in us. These are very different states. When God lives in us, we should abandon ourselves completely to him, but when we live in him, we have to take care to employ every possible means to achieve a complete surrender to him. These means are clear enough: courses of reading, self-analysis, regular examination of our progress—everything is done by rule. Even the hours for conversation are fixed, and a spiritual director is always available. But when God lives in us, we have nothing to help us beyond what he gives us moment by moment. Nothing else is provided and no road is marked out. We are like a child who can be led about wherever one wishes and who is ignorant of everything except what is put in front of it. We are given no books with carefully marked passages, and very often we have no regular director, for God leaves us without any support except himself. We are abandoned and live in darkness. We are forgotten. Death and nothingness are our portion. We are aware of our needs and of our wretchedness, but we do not know from where or if any help will come. Meanwhile we do not worry and we wait quietly for someone to come and help us, and we keep our thoughts fixed on heaven.

God sees nothing better in us than this total resignation of ourselves, and he himself provides us with books, gives us insight into our souls, together with advice and examples from the lives of the good and wise. Other people have great difficulty in discovering spiritual truths, but we, who have given ourselves to God, have no trouble. These others hold on to their spiritual discoveries, keep coming back and brooding over them, but we in whom God lives seize what each moment brings and then forget it, eager only to be alert to respond to God and live for him alone. They who live in God perform countless good works for his glory, but those in whom God lives are often flung into a corner like a useless bit of broken pottery. There they lie, forsaken by everyone, but yet enjoying God's very real and active love and knowing they have to do nothing but stay in his hands and be used as he wishes. Often they have no idea how they will be used, but he knows. The world thinks them useless and it seems as if they are. Yet it is quite certain that by various means and through hidden channels they pour out spiritual help on people who are often quite unaware of it and of whom they themselves never think. For those who have surrendered themselves completely to God, all they are and do has power. Their lives are sermons. They are apostles. God gives a special force to all they say and do, even to their silence, their tranquillity and their detachment, which, quite unknown to them, profoundly influences other people. They themselves are influenced by others who by grace unknowingly benefit them; and, in turn, they are used to guide and support other people who have no direct connection with them. God works through them by unexpected and hidden impulses. In this respect, they are like Jesus, who produced a secret healing power. The difference between him and them is that they are often unaware of this discharge of power and so do not co-operate with it. It is like a hidden scent which gives off its sweetness unknowingly and is quite ignorant of its strength.

(2) *How God guides the soul through every kind of obscurity.*

The moment the soul comes closely under the influence of God, it forsakes all its good works, its devotional practices, its methods of prayer, its books, its ideas and its discussions with other religious persons so that it can be alone and rely on the guidance of God, which is, henceforth, the unique source of its holiness. It is in his hands, as the saints have always been, realizing that God alone knows what is right for it, and that if it relied on human guidance it would inevitably lose its way in that unknown land into which God conducts it. It is the will of God which guides souls along paths which it alone knows.

When the wind is shifting, one can be sure of its direction only from moment to moment. So it is with these souls. They too have their course continually altered by the will of God, and his will can be understood only by its effects, by what it accomplishes in these souls either through secret, hidden promptings or through the duties of their state of life. This is all the spiritual knowledge they have; it is the sum total of their visions and revelations, all their wisdom and instruction. They need nothing more. Faith assures them that what they do is good. If they read, talk, write or seek advice, it is only to enable them to recognize God's will more clearly. They accept all these means as part of God's activity, but do not become attached to them. By faith they are every moment upheld by the infallible, unchanging and always effective power of God. This power they perceive and enjoy in all things, from the smallest to the greatest, and it serves them continually. They make use of things, not that they have any confidence in them, but because they are submissive to God's will, which they find active in the most unlikely situations. And so they pass their lives without squandering it in vain study and equally vain longings. Nor do they find anything tedious in life or anything to complain about, for they have a settled assurance that they are following the most perfect way. They enjoy supreme bliss because they see the fullness of God's power being exercised in whatever conditions of body or soul they find themselves, in whatever happens to them internally or externally and in whatever befalls them at each and every moment. Whatever the world offers them is nothing. They judge all things by God's standards. If he takes from them their powers of thought and speech, their books, their food, their friends, their health, and even life itself, it means no more to them than if he did the exact opposite. They love all he does and find his activity always sanctifying. They do not reason about what he does, but approve of it. They know it is never without significance.

(3) *Abandonment contains in itself pure faith, hope and love.*

This state of abandonment is a blending of faith, hope and love in one single act which unites us to God and all his activities. When these three virtues are united, they of course become one and so form a single act, a single raising of the heart to God and a simple abandonment to him. How can we explain this divine blending, this spiritual oneness? How can we give a name which will give an idea of its nature and make the unity of this trinity comprehensible? Well, those three virtues enable us to possess and enjoy, in one single impulse, God and his will. We see and love him and hope to receive all things from him. We can call this attitude one of pure love, pure hope or pure faith. Now, we usually designate this state under the name of pure faith, but it must be understood that this term includes the other theological virtues. God makes certain that nothing is more secure than this state, and our hearts are completely disinterested. In this union there is on God's side the absolute certitude of faith, and in our hearts a similar certitude but one tinged with fear and hope.

What a desirable unity is the trinity of these most excellent virtues! So let us believe, hope and love, because of the simple prompting of the Holy Spirit. Then the fervor inspired by the name of God will be diffused throughout our whole being by the Holy Spirit. Here is this mystical revelation, this pledge of predestination with all its happy results. "God is indeed good to Israel, the Lord is good to pure hearts" (Ps. 73:1). This caress of the Holy Spirit on souls influenced by love is called pure love because of the torrent of delight which sweeps over them, bringing with it an abundance of faith and insight. But when souls are living in distress it is called pure faith, because all they know is the pitch-black darkness of the night. Pure love sees, feels and believes. Pure faith believes, though it neither sees nor feels. That is the difference between these two states. Yet this difference is not fundamental, for the condition of pure faith is not without love, nor is pure love lacking in faith or abandonment. The divine touch can blend these three virtues differently and create all the varieties of spiritual conditions; and as God can arrange them in an infinite diversity, there is not a single soul which is not given the divine imprint in a way which best suits its own individuality. But this is not important. This imprint is always made up of faith, hope and love. Self-abandonment is the normal means of securing special virtues. We cannot all hope that God will give us the same sort of virtue nor lift us to the same state, but we can all be united with God, we can all abandon ourselves to his will, we can all receive from him what is most fitting for us and, at last, we can all find the kingdom of God, and share in his glory. In this kingdom we can all seek for a crown of love or a crown of faith. It does not matter which. It is still a crown and, always, the kingdom of God. It is true there is a difference. Some of us will live in the shadows and some of us in the full light of day. But what on earth does it matter as long as we belong to God and obey his will? Surely we shall not trouble ourselves about the technical name of the state in which we find ourselves, nor what its splendors are. Of course not. We seek God alone. All else is irrelevant. We should stop preaching to souls about the state of pure faith or of pure love, about the cross or the sweetness of religion, for everyone is very different and these matters may be unsuitable for them. Instead, let us tell everyone who loves God about self-abandonment to the divine action in general and make them understand that by this they will achieve that particular state chosen and destined for them from all eternity. Let us not dishearten, nor rebuff, nor drive away a single soul from seeking that high perfection to which Jesus calls everyone. He demands that all of us submit to the will of his Father and so form his mystical body, whose members cannot truthfully call him their head unless their wills are in perfect accordance with his. Let us never stop telling people that this gentle and loving Savior never asks anything from them that is difficult or any extraordinary labors. He wishes only that they desire to be united with him so that he can guide, direct and befriend them in proportion to the closeness of that union.

(4) *Abandonment involves the most heroic generosity.*

There is nothing more generous than a soul which, afire with faith, sees only the working of God in all troubles and the most deadly dangers. It may be a matter of drinking poison, marching into the breach, or working like a slave for the plague-stricken. In all such things the soul finds the fullness of divine life, not offered drop by drop, but engulfing it instantly. An army of soldiers with such a spirit would be invincible. For faith lifts and expands the heart above and beyond all that the senses fear. The life of faith and the instinct of faith are one and the same thing. It is delight in the friendship of God and confidence in his protection which makes everything acceptable and to be received with good grace. Faith also produces a certain detachment of soul which enables us to handle any situation and every kind of person. With faith we are never unhappy and never weak. The soul, with its living faith in God, always sees him acting behind happenings which bewilder our senses. Stricken with terror, our senses suddenly cry to the soul: "Unhappy wretch, now you are lost and there's no hope of rescue!" The robust voice of faith instantly replies: "Hold fast, go forward and fear nothing."

(5) *Abandonment and pure faith do more for the soul than good works.*

We can find astonishing things in the stories of the saints—revelations, visions and interior voices—but they are only a glimpse of the perfection which is hidden in their life of faith. For their faith contains all these happenings, since those who live by it know how to recognize God in everything that occurs from moment to moment. When these supernatural favors bestowed upon a saint become apparent to others, it does not imply that the saint has not already enjoyed them. What it means is that these favors are disclosed in order to illuminate his virtue and persuade other souls to imitate it. The glories of Thabor and the miracles of Jesus Christ were not mere sideshows. They were flashes of light which from time to time broke through the dark cloud of his humanity so that it could be recognized and loved.

The wonderful thing about the saints is that their faith never wavers. Without this they would not be saints. Their living faith in God, which enables them to rejoice in the fact that he manifests himself in everything, has no need of any external marvels. They could be useful only if other people needed to be convinced by such signs. But for himself, the saint, steeped in faith and happy in his obscurity, has no need of them. They are allowed to become visible for the benefit of those who may profit by them, but for himself the saint cherishes what we can all experience: the will of God which works in secret and does not show itself openly. Faith wants no proofs, and those who demand them are lacking in faith. They who live by faith will receive proofs, not as such but as favors from God, and there is really nothing contradictory between these extraordinary things and the state of pure faith. Many saints are raised up by God for the salvation of souls and to enlighten the most backward. Such saints were the prophets and the apostles and all those others who have been and will be chosen by God to illuminate the world. There will always be such saints, as there have always been. But there is also a multitude of others hidden in the bosom of the Church who are destined to shine only in heaven, and so in this life they live and die in complete obscurity.

(6) *Abandonment contains within itself the virtues of all other spiritual exercises.*

When our hearts are truly abandoned, we embrace every possible kind of spirituality, for our whole being gives itself up to God's will, and this act of surrender, prompted by pure love, means that we involve ourselves in all that pleases him. There is not a moment when we are not abandoned without the slightest reservation, and so, inevitably, the nature of this abandonment comprises every variety of the spiritual life.

So it is no business of ours to decide what our submission to God will bring to us. All we must do is submit to everything and be ready for every possibility. In this free offering of the soul to God he demands three things: renunciation, obedience and love. Everything else is his affair. If we carefully fulfill the duties imposed on us by our state of life, if we quietly follow any impulse coming from God, if we peacefully submit to the influence of grace, we are making an act of total abandonment. It is one that is not limited in any way, but has all the value and the effectiveness which sincere good will always has, even though what it seeks to do is beyond its control. What we have wanted to do is done in the sight of God.

It may please God to limit the exercise of our various talents, but he never puts any check on the exercise of our will. God's purposes, his being, his essence are the objects of our will and love, and, because of this, he ensures that our union with him is full and complete. From time to time our love may direct our faculties to particular and immediate ends. That is because God's will is concerned with those same ends and he limits its operation, as it were, to the demands of the present moment; but as he animates our faculties he enters our hearts. When he finds them pure and free of all reserve, he fills them with himself, for, being emptied of all things, our hearts have an infinite capacity and so are able to receive him. O holy detachment! It is you who makes room for God! O purity! O complete surrender! It is you who draw God into my heart! I care nothing about my capabilities and talents. You, Lord, are all I want or need. Use this little creature as you wish. All is yours, all is from you and all is for you. I have no longer anything to look after or to do. Not a single moment is controlled by me, for everything is yours. I have not to try to add anything to my stature or take anything away; nor have I to inquire into or reflect upon anything. It is for you to deal with everything. Holiness, perfection, salvation, spiritual direction, penance—these are all your business. Mine is to be content with you and not adopt any line of action or involve myself in any attachment, but to leave all to your good pleasure.

(7) *Everyone is called to enjoy the infinite benefits of
this state.*

This is why I preach self-abandonment and not any particular way of life. I love whatever is the state in which your
grace places souls and have no liking for one more than
another. I teach all souls a general method by which they
can attain that state you have designed for them. I ask of
them nothing but an eagerness to abandon themselves completely to your guidance, for you will lead them very surely
to what is best for them. It is faith I preach to them: abandonment, confidence and faith. They must long to be subject
to and the tool of God's action, believing that at every moment and through all things this action is at work for them
according to the measure of their good will. This is the faith
I preach. It is not a special state of faith and pure love, but a
general one by which all souls can find God in whatever
guise he assumes and can take that form which his grace has
ready for them. I am speaking to all kinds of souls. My deepest instinct is to belong to everyone, to proclaim to all the
secret of the Gospel, and to be "all things to all men" (I Cor.
9:22). Having this fortunate temperament, I make it my
duty—which I find an easy one—to "rejoice with those who
rejoice and be sad with those in sorrow" (Rom. 12:15), to
speak to simpletons in their own language and to use the
speech of scholars when talking to learned men. I want to
make it clear to everyone that not all can hope for the same
special favors, but they can all attain to the same love, the
same abandonment and the same God, and so can all, without
distinction, reach the heights of holiness. Extraordinary favors
and privileges are called thus because there are so few souls
faithful enough to merit them. This will be seen very clearly
on the day of judgment. Alas! it will then be found that
these favors were not withheld by God, but that souls
were deprived of them entirely through their own fault. What a
flood of blessings they would have enjoyed if their submission had been total and unwavering!
    It is exactly the same with Jesus and souls. Those who had

no trust in him or respect for him received none of the favors which he offered everyone. For that, they had only their own wicked dispositions to blame. It is true that not everyone can soar to the same sublime heights, obtain the same gifts and achieve the same degree of perfection. But if we all were faithful to grace and responded to it according to our abilities, we should all be satisfied, because we should reach a measure of excellence and place in God's favor that would completely satisfy our desires. We should be well content, according to nature and according to grace, for nature and grace share an equal longing for this blessed state.

(8) *A pure heart and perfect abandonment bring us all the treasures of grace.*

If we wish to enjoy an abundance of blessings we have only one thing to do: purify our hearts by emptying them of all desire for created things and surrender ourselves wholly to God. By doing this we shall get all we want. Let others, Lord, ask you for all sorts of gifts. Let them increase their prayers and entreaties. But I, my Lord, ask for one thing only and have only a single prayer—give me a pure heart! How happy we are if our hearts are pure! Through the ardor of our faith we see God as he is. We see him in everything and at every moment working within and around us. And in all things we are both his subject and his instrument. He guides us everywhere and leads us to everything. Very often we do not think about it, but he thinks for us. It is enough that we have desired what is happening to us and must happen to us by his will. He understands our readiness. We are bewildered and seek to find this desire within ourselves, but we cannot. He, though, sees it very clearly. How silly we are! Surely we know what a well-disposed heart is: one where God is found. He sees all the good intentions there and consequently knows that this heart will always be submissive to his will. He is also aware that we do not know what is useful for us, so he makes it his business to give it to us. He cares nothing about thwarting us. If we are going eastward, he makes us turn to the west. If we are about to run onto the rocks, he takes the helm and brings us into port. We have neither map nor compass, know nothing of winds or tides, yet we always make a prosperous voyage. If pirates try to board us, an unexpected gust of wind sweeps us beyond their reach.

Good will and a pure heart! Jesus well knew what he was doing when he set you among the Beatitudes. Can there be a greater happiness than to possess God if he also possesses us? It is a state of charmed delight in which the soul sleeps peacefully in the bosom of providence, plays innocently with the divine wisdom (Prov. 8:30), and feels no anxiety about the voyage which continues on its even, happy way in spite of rocks and pirates and continual storms.

A pure heart and good will! The one foundation of every spiritual state! On you are bestowed and by you are made profitable the gifts of pure faith, pure hope, pure confidence and pure love. On your trunk are grafted the flowers of the desert, those precious graces which blossom in those completely detached souls in whom, as if in a deserted place, God makes his dwelling to the exclusion of all else. You are the wellspring from which flow all the rivulets that water the flowerpots of the bridegroom and the garden of the bride. The pure heart could well say to every soul: "Look at me carefully. It is I who generate that love which chooses the better part and clings to it, I who produce that mild but effective fear which arouses such a detestation of evil that it can easily be avoided, I who impart that excellent understanding which reveals the greatness of God and the merit of virtue. And it is also I who cause that passionate and holy yearning which keeps the soul resolute in virtue in the expectation of that enjoyment of God which will one day, more perfectly than now, be the delight of every faithful soul. Yes, O pure Heart, you can invite everyone to gather round you and enrich themselves with your inexhaustible treasures. There is not one single kind of spiritual activity, not one path to holiness which does not lead back to you. From you they derive all that is beautiful, attractive and delightful. They draw everything from you. Those marvelous fruits of grace and goodness, which we see all around us and nourish us, come from the trees and bushes transplanted into your most fertile garden. Your land flows with milk and honey (Ecclus. 46:8). Milk comes from your breasts, and your bosom is perfumed with myrrh (Song of Songs 1:13).

Come, then, my beloved souls, let us run and fly to that love which calls us. Why are we waiting? Let us set out at once, lose ourselves in the very heart of God and become intoxicated with his love. Let us snatch from his heart the key to all the treasures of heaven and then start out right away on the road to heaven. There is no need to fear that anything will be locked against us. Our key will open every door. There is no room we cannot enter. We can make ourselves free of the garden, the cellar and the vineyard. If we want to explore the countryside, no one will hinder us. We can come and go, enter and leave anyplace we want to because we have the key of David (Rev. 3:7), the key of knowledge (Luke 11:52), the key of the abyss (Rev. 9:1), in which are all the hidden treasures of the divine wisdom (Wis. 8:14). It is this key which opens the doors of mystical death and its sacred darkness. By it we can enter the deepest dungeons and emerge safe and sound. It gives us entrance into that blessed spot where the light of knowledge shines and the bridegroom takes his noonday rest (Song of Songs 1:7). There we quickly learn how to win his kiss (Song of Songs 1:1) and ascend with confidence the steps of the nuptial couch and learn there the secrets of love—divine secrets which must not be revealed and which no human tongue can describe.

So, dear souls, let us love, for love will give us everything. It gives us holiness and all that accompanies it. It is all around us and flows into every receptive heart. O what a thing is this holy seed which ripens into eternal life! We cannot praise it enough. But why even speak about it? How much better it is to possess it in silence than praise it in wholly inadequate words. But what am I saying? We must praise this love, but only because we are possessed by it, for, from the very moment it seizes us, reading, writing, speaking and everything else mean nothing to us. We can take or leave anything, we can stay at home or go out into the marketplace, we can be fighting fit or ill, dull or lively—according to what the heart dictates. For this love-filled heart governs the rest of us. We are a mixture of the flesh and the spirit, and the heart reigns supreme over both, and all that is inspired by love delights it. But anything which unredeemed nature or the devil puts forward fills it with disgust and horror. If it is sometimes taken by surprise, it means that it will be wiser and more humble in the future.

CHAPTER IV

COMPLETE SURRENDER TO THE WILL
OF GOD IS THE ESSENCE OF
SPIRITUALITY

(1) *The complete and entire surrender of themselves to
God is the supreme duty of souls called by him to
the state of abandonment.*

"Offer sacrifice in the right spirit and trust in the Lord"
(Ps. 4:5). Which is to say that the great and firm foundation of the spiritual life is the offering of ourselves to God and
being subject to his will in all things. We must completely
forget ourselves, so that we regard ourselves as an object
which has been sold and over which we no longer have
any rights. We find all our joy in fulfilling God's pleasure—
his happiness, his glory and the fact that he is our great and
only delight. Once we have this foundation, all we need to do
is spend our lives rejoicing that God is God and being so
wholly abandoned to his will that we are quite indifferent as
to what we do and equally indifferent as to what use he makes
of our activities. Our main duty is to abandon ourselves, once
we have faithfully discharged all the proper duties of our
state of life, of course, for the way in which we fulfill these
duties will be the measure of our holiness.

A holy soul is one which, by the help of grace, has freely
submitted to God's will, and all that follows this free consent
is the work of God and never that of man, who blindly abandons himself and is completely indifferent about everything.
That is all God asks of us. In everything else he arranges
and chooses all things as an architect plans a building. So it
is essential that we should love God and his designs however they are presented to us. They are nothing to do with
us. They are a matter for God alone, and what he gives is

best for us. The essence of spirituality is contained in this phrase: "complete and utter abandonment to the will of God." By that I mean we should never think of ourselves, but be continually occupied with loving and obeying him. We must put aside all those fears, those uneasy broodings, those qualms of conscience, and those anxieties which can arise from the concern we have for achieving holiness and our salvation. As God wants to look after all our affairs, let us leave them all to him so that we can concentrate our whole attention on him. So come! With heads erect, let us advance, ignoring everything, and remaining always satisfied with God and with all that he makes us do and accomplishes within us. Let us take good care not to get foolishly involved in all those fears and doubts which, like paths leading nowhere, only tempt us to wander on and on until we are hopelessly lost. Let us leap over this maze of self-love instead of trying to explore its endless alleys.

So come! Never mind weariness, illness, lack of feeling, irritability, exhaustion, the snares of the devil and of men, with all that they create of distrust, jealousy, prejudice and evil imaginings. Let us soar like an eagle above these clouds, with our eyes fixed on the sun and its rays, which are our duties. We cannot help being aware of all these evils, of course, and we cannot be indifferent to them, but let us never forget that ours is not a life governed by our feelings. We must live in those upper reaches of the spiritual life where God and his will are active in a process which is eternal and unchanging. There, he who is uncreated, immeasurable and cannot be described by human words, will keep us far removed from all the shadows and turmoil of the world. We shall feel through our senses countless disturbances, it is true, but they will all disappear like the clouds in a windswept sky. God and his will are the eternal objects which captivate every faithful soul, and when the day of glory arrives, they will be our true happiness. Here on earth we suffer—to use the language of allegory—the attacks of monsters, owls and savage beasts. But terrible though these attacks are, behind them God is acting and giving us something of the divine which will give us the brilliance of the sun, for here below both body and soul are refined and fashioned like gold and iron, linen and gems. Like these things, they will not attain their full beauty until they have been trimmed and shaped and changed from their original form. All they have endured in this life at the hand of God—and he is love itself—is meant only to prepare them for eternal bliss. The truly faithful soul, well versed in all the secrets of God, lives in peace, and, instead of being frightened by what happens to it, is com- forted, for it is quite, quite certain that God is guiding it. It accepts all things as a manifestation of God's grace, ignores itself and thinks only of what God is doing. Love inspires it to perform its duties most carefully and faithfully. A soul com- pletely abandoned to God sees nothing clearly except the action of grace, apart, that is, from those slight defects which grace can turn to good account.

(2)   *If we wish to reach the state of abandonment, we must get rid of any love for created things.*

No thought, no mental effort will teach us anything about pure love. We can learn of it only through the activity of God, and God teaches us, both through our reason and through difficulties and setbacks. What we learn by these teachings is that there is nothing good except God. To know this we must get rid of all we hold dear. We must strip ourselves of every- thing. We cannot be settled in the state of pure love until we have experienced a lot of setbacks and many humiliations. We must reach the stage when all that the world contains ceases to exist and God is everything to us. Now for this to happen, God destroys all our personal affections. It does not matter what they are. We may take up some special kind of devotion, a particular pious practice, try to become perfect by following certain paths and seek the guidance of other people. No matter what it is we attach ourselves to, God will step in and upset our plans so that, instead of peace, we shall find ourselves in the midst of confusion, trouble and folly. As soon as we say, "I must go this way, I must con- sult this person, I must act like this," God at once says the opposite and withdraws his power from those means which we ourselves have chosen. So we discover the emptiness of all created things, are forced to turn to God and be content with him.

How fortunate we are if we understand God's loving strictness and eagerly co-operate with it. We rise above all that passes away and repose in the unchanging and the infinite, and no longer put our trust in created things, but have dealings with them only when God wills it. God sees that we are empty of all our own desires and unable to make our own choice. We are dead and buried in complete indifference. When God in all his fullness comes and fills our hearts, he casts over all created things an annihilating shadow which blots out all their differences and variety. So these creatures lack all power to accomplish anything and we feel no attraction to them, for the majesty of God fills our hearts to overflowing. Dwelling in God, we are dead to all things, and all things are dead to us. It is the concern of God, who gives life to everything, to restore our souls to life in regard to what he has created and then, by his will, we can approach his creatures and our souls can accept them. Without the action of his will, we shall reject them and feel no interest in them. This annihilation of all creatures, and then their restoration to serve the designs of God, ensures that each moment God is both himself and all things to us. For at each moment our hearts are at peace in God and completely abandoned to all creation. Therefore each of these moments contains all things.

(3) *The active exercise of abandonment.*

Those souls called by God to the state of self-abandonment are far more passive than active, yet they cannot expect to be relieved from all activity. This state is nothing but an intensification of the normal virtue of abandonment by being practiced more regularly and more perfectly. Thus we have two duties to fulfill: we must actively seek to carry God's will into effect and passively accept all that his will sends us. As I have already said, this state is essentially the gift of our entire being to God for him to use as he pleases. Now he uses us in two ways. He either forces us to do certain things, or he acts within us. In the first case we must unhesitatingly obey his clear and obvious orders; in the second, we must submit with absolute docility to what he is doing within our souls. Self-abandonment implies all this, for it is the perfect submission to God's will as it reveals itself moment by moment. It is of no consequence to us to know how we have to abandon ourselves nor what each moment will bring. But what is of supreme importance is that we should abandon ourselves without reserve.

So there are duties which are ordered and must be done. There is also the duty of remaining quite passive and abandoned. And there is a third type of duty—obeying those promptings with which God moves all of us who are submissive to him. To perform this last duty we must have a great deal of simplicity, a gentle cheerfulness, and we must also respond at once to the breath of grace. We must let ourselves go, ready and eager to obey our impulses, for God never fails to give us guidance to tell us what we may accept or reject among these influences. This third kind of duty is governed by no rules or formalities, and it is this duty which produces what, when we consider the saints, appears to us unusual and extraordinary and which governs their vocal prayer and their interior aspirations and lights up their lives with their austerities, their warmth and their unsparing sacrifices for their neighbor. All this comes under the control of the Holy Spirit, so we should not seek to have these graces or complain that we cannot be remarkable in our virtues, for all depends on the will of God. Unless we accept this, it is likely we shall follow our own wills and be deluded. We should observe here that there are some souls whom God wishes to keep hidden, obscure and negligible both to themselves and others, and far from giving them any outstanding qualities, he allows them none. They would be mistaken if they sought to advance along any other path, and if they are properly instructed they will realize that they must be faithful to the part allotted them and find peace in their lowliness. The only difference between them and other souls is that they create by their love of God a submission to his will, for if in these they surpass souls who seem to be active in exterior works, their holiness will certainly be deeper. This shows that we should be content with the duties of our state and the orders of providence, for it is clear that God demands this from all of us. We ourselves must not try to produce spiritual pleasures and experiences, nor try to intensify those we may have. Such natural efforts are in direct opposition and quite contrary to the inspirations of the Holy Spirit. It is the bridegroom's voice which should awaken the soul, which will move only as moved by him. Should the soul act on its own, it will accomplish nothing. If we feel neither desire nor ability to perform marvels similar to those which make the saints so admirable, we should, in justice to ourselves, say: "God wants these things from the saints, but not from me."

(4) *How those people live who have been called to the state of abandonment.*

It seems to me that such people's lives are similar to those of Jesus, the Blessed Virgin and St. Joseph. Such a life is one of complete dependence on God's good pleasure and one of complete inertia until stirred by his will. The thing that must be noted about this will is that, to use human expressions, it seems to be casual and haphazard in its operation. I shall call it the purely providential will of God, to distinguish it from that other aspect of his will which imposes definite obligations we must fulfill. Leaving aside this manifestation of his will, the people I am talking about are wholly subject to his providential will. So their lives, although really extraordinary, show nothing which is not quite usual and ordinary. They fulfill all the duties of religion and all those inherent in their way of life, just as others apparently do. We can investigate them closely but we shall find nothing special or striking about them. Their lives seem commonplace. Anything which might single them out is not apparent. It is their dependence on God's will which settles everything for them. Because of the continual submission of their hearts, this will gives complete self-mastery. Whether they co-operate consciously with it or obey it without even noticing they are doing so, is all one. God uses them to help other souls.

They are, by their state, solitary and free, detached from all things, satisfied to love God peacefully, belong to him and accomplish faithfully the immediate task in conformity with his will. There is no reflection, no looking back, no consideration of consequences or the whys and the wherefores. It is enough for them to go on unaffectedly and do their obvious duty as if nothing in the world existed except God and it. The present moment is like a desert in which these uncomplicated souls see and enjoy only God and attend to nothing but his will. Everything else is ignored, forgotten and left to providence. They are like an instrument which only accepts or acts according to whether it is passively occupied with God's purpose or directed by him to some outside activity. Now this exterior activity is accompanied by a free and lively co-operation, yet one that is infused and mystical. That is to say that God, finding that these souls are tuned up and ready to act if he gives the word, is well-satisfied and spares them the need for action, but yet grants them all the benefits they would have gained by their efforts and good will. It is as if someone who sees a friend preparing to go on a journey on his behalf immediately assumes his friend's appearance and makes the journey himself; so, in fact, all this friend has done is show his willingness to go, for the actual trip was made by someone else. This journey would not be a forced one, because it would be the result of a free decision to serve a person who then undertook the labor and cost of the journey; it would be an active one, for the journey would really be made; yet it would be an interior one, since it would be performed without any activity on the friend's part; and it would be a mystical one, for the truth about the journey would be hidden.

We should note that the kind of co-operation involved in this imaginary journey is entirely different from the obedience with which we carry out our normal duties. The work by which we fulfill these duties is neither mystical nor infused, but free and active in the common meaning of the words. Abandonment to God's will is both active and passive. When we abandon ourselves we provide nothing of our own apart from a habitual broad good will, which works for nothing but is ready for anything. We are like a tool which is quite useless until it is in the hands of a workman, where it performs all the tasks for which it was designed. But obedience to the clearly expressed and definite will of God is a different matter. It implies normal vigilance, care, prudence and discretion. Grace may help us. Leave everything else to God, except for your love and obedience to the duties of the present moment. This love is a very real act and is an inescapable obligation. We must cherish it ceaselessly and always be ready to obey its promptings, which obviously we cannot do without acting. The instant response to our immediate duties is, of course, also action. It is action by which we fulfill God's will made apparent to us by external situations and events, although we expect to see nothing extraordinary in them. This is for us the one law, the one supreme rule, the one clear and certain path. It is a law which is unchanged by place, time and circumstances. It is a straight line which we must follow undeviatingly, with faith and courage and without any questioning. To sum up: we must be active in all that the present moment demands of us, but in everything else remain passive and abandoned and do nothing but peacefully await the promptings of God.

(5)   *If we wish to be united to God we should value all the operations of his grace, but we should cling only to the duties of the present moment.*

We possess and enjoy God by union with his will, and we deceive ourselves if we imagine we can have this delight by any other means. Union with his will is the unique means. There is no special way of achieving this, for he can ensure it by any means he wants. God unites his will to ours in a thousand different ways, and the one he employs in our case is always the best for us. We should honor and love them all, for they are all arranged by God to suit each individual soul to bring about this union. We must hold fast to what he chooses and make no choice for ourselves, yet be eager to revere and love whatever he fixes upon for other people. For instance, if God wants me to use vocal prayers and enjoy spiritually moving devotions, I should still love and venerate the silence and the dark night which the faith of others brings them. But, as far as I am concerned, I shall use the duties of the present moment and by them be united with God. I shall not, as the Quietists do, believe that true religion means doing nothing, for we become holy by the law of God, and he always makes all he chooses useful to us. No, I shall not attempt to set limits to the will of God. I shall welcome it however it manifests itself, and shall rejoice to see it working on others, no matter what form it takes. So paradoxical though it sounds, we all have only one way to perfection, but within that way there are certain differences and variations to suit our individualities. And all of us, if we have the needful simplicity, say: "Let us keep going toward the same goal but by our own path, united in our obedience to God, who manifests his will so differently to each of us." It is with this in mind that we should read the lives of saints and other books of spirituality, without ever leaving the path allotted to us. This is why we should never read spiritual books or talk with other people about spiritual matters unless God permits us to. But if he does make it clear that it is our immediate duty to do this, we shall not change course, but rather be established in it no matter what we read or discuss. But if what we read and discuss is not planned for us by God to meet the needs of the present moment, we shall have nothing but trouble and confusion, because without God's will there can be only turmoil. So why do we become troubled and anxious about matters which have nothing to do with what we should do here and now? When will God be all in all to us? Let us live entirely for God.

(6) *From abandoned souls, God demands complete surrender to his grace.*

We must keep ourselves detached from all we feel or do if we are to travel along his path and live only for God and the duties of the present moment. We must stop all imaginings about the future, keep our attention on what is happening now and not bother about anything that has gone before or what may follow. I imagine that God's will always governs you. You will then have some inner prompting which makes you say: "I feel drawn toward this person or this book; I would like to give another person some advice or ask for some myself; I wish to complain about something, to open my heart to someone and in turn receive confidence, to give something away or to perform a certain action." We should at once obey these promptings of grace without relying on our reason or considering the matter at all. We must give ourselves to whatever God wishes and for as long as he wishes and yet never get personally involved in them. In this condition of self-abandonment the will of God moves us because he dwells within us, and it should completely replace everything on which we usually rely for strength and support. There is never a moment when there is not some virtue to be practiced, and, as abandoned souls, we shall remember all that we have learned through reading and discussion so that the most obedient of novices could not fulfill her duties better. This is why we are sometimes impelled to read various books, and prompted to make some comment and give our opinion on the most trifling matter. At one moment God gives us the desire to instruct ourselves in what, at a later moment, will help us to act virtuously. But whatever we do, we do it because we are drawn to this particular action without knowing why. All we can say can be reduced to this: "I feel drawn to write, to read, to question and examine. I obey this feeling, and God, who is responsible for it, thus builds up within me a kind of spiritual store which, in the future, will develop into a core of usefulness for myself and for others." This is what makes it essential for us to be simple-hearted, gentle, compliant and sensitive to the slightest breath of these almost imperceptible promptings.

If we have abandoned ourselves, there is only one rule for us: the duty of the present moment. The soul is as light as a feather, as fluid as water, simple as a child and as lively as a ball in responding to all the impulses of grace. We are like molten metal which takes the shape of the mold into which it is poured, and can just as easily assume any form God wishes to give us. We are like the air which stirs continually, or water which fills every vessel no matter what its shape.

We must offer ourselves to God like a clean, smooth canvas

and not worry ourselves about what God may choose to paint on it, for we have perfect trust in him, have abandoned ourselves to him, and are so busy doing our duty that we forget ourselves and all our needs. The more closely we devote ourselves to our little task, which is so simple, so secret and so hidden and apparently so paltry, the more does God enrich and adorn it: "God works wonders for those he loves" (Ps. 4:3).

It is true that a canvas simply and blindly offered to the brush feels at each moment only the stroke of the brush. It is the same with a lump of stone. Each blow from the hammering of the sculptor's chisel makes it feel—if it could—as if it were being destroyed. As blow after blow descends, the stone knows nothing of how the sculptor is shaping it. All it feels is a chisel chopping away at it, cutting it and mutilating it. For example, let's take a piece of stone destined to be carved into a crucifix or a statue. We might ask it: "What do you think is happening to you?" And it might answer: "Don't ask me. All I know is that I must stay immovable in the hands of the sculptor, and I must love him and endure all he inflicts on me to produce the figure he has in mind. He knows how to do it. As for me, I have no idea what he is doing, nor do I know what he will make of me. But what I do know is that his work is the best possible. It is perfect. I welcome each blow of his chisel as the best thing that could happen to me, although, if I'm to be truthful, I feel that every one of these blows is ruining me, destroying me and disfiguring me. But I remain unconcerned. I concentrate on the present moment, think only of my duty, and suffer all that this master sculptor inflicts on me without knowing his purpose or fretting about it."

Yes, you frank and precious souls, leave to God what is his business and carry on peacefully with your work. Be quite sure that whatever happens to your spiritual life or to your activities in the world is always for the best. Let God act, and abandon yourself to him. Let the chisel and the brush do their work, even though the brush covers the canvas with so many colors that, instead of a picture, it seems there is only a daub. Let us work together with the will of God by a steady and simple submission, a complete forgetfulness of self and concentration on our duties. Let us go straight ahead. Never mind the lack of a map, ignore the lie of the land and take no notice of the places you pass through. Keep going and you will attain all you desire. Everything will be given to you if, with love and obedience, you seek God's kingdom and his right-eousness. There are many people who are uneasy and ask: "Who will guide us toward that mortification of self which will lead us to perfect holiness?" Well, leave them to ran-sack books in an effort to find a formula to help them. Let us stay united with God by love and let us walk blindly along the clear straight path of duty. His angels protect you, and if he wants more from you he will let you know.

(7) *If we are truly docile, we shall ask no questions about the road along which God is taking us.*

When God becomes our guide he insists that we trust him without reservations and put aside all nervousness about his guidance. We are sent along the path he has chosen for us, but we cannot see it, and nothing we have read is any help to us. Were we acting on our own we should have to rely on our experience. It would be too risky to do anything else. But it is very different when God acts with us. Divine action is al-ways new and fresh, it never retraces its steps, but always finds new routes. When we are led by this action, we have no idea where we are going, for the paths we tread cannot be discovered from books or by any of our thoughts. But these paths are always opened in front of us and we are impelled along them. Imagine we are in a strange district at night and are crossing fields unmarked by any path, but we have a guide. He asks no advice nor tells us of his plans. So what can we do except trust him? It is no use trying to see where we are, look at maps, or question passers-by. That would not be tolerated by a guide who wants us to rely on him. He will get satisfac-tion from overcoming our fears and doubts, and will insist that we have complete trust in him.

God's activity can never be anything but good, and does not need to be reformed or controlled. It began at the crea-tion of the world and up to now has continued with the same energy, which knows no limits. Its fertility is inexhaustible. It does one thing today, another tomorrow, yet it is the same activity which every moment produces constantly fresh results, and it will continue throughout eternity. It produced Abel, Noah and Abraham—all different types. Isaac is also original. Jacob is not a duplicate of him, nor is Joseph a facsimile of Jacob. Moses is different from his ancestors. David and the prophets bear no resemblance to the patriarchs. John the Baptist stands alone. Jesus Christ is the first-born, and the Apostles are moved more by the guidance of his spirit than by imitating his works. Jesus Christ did not restrict himself, for he did not follow all his own precepts literally. His most holy soul was always inspired by the Holy Spirit and always responsive to its slightest breath. He never had to consult the moment that had passed to know what to do in the coming one, for his every moment was conditioned by the breath of grace according to those eternal truths contained in the invisible and unfathomable wisdom of the Holy Trinity. His soul received its orders constantly and carried them out in his daily life. The Gospel lets us see the effect of these truths in the life of Jesus Christ, and it is this same Jesus Christ, always alive and active, who continues to live and work fresh wonders in the souls of those who love him.

If we wish to live according to the Gospel, we must abandon ourselves simply and completely to the action of God. Jesus Christ is its source. He "is the same today as he was yesterday and as he will be forever" (Heb. 13:8). What he has done is finished, what remains to be done is being carried on every moment. Every saint shares in this divine life, and Jesus Christ, though always the same, is different in each one. The life of each saint is the life of Jesus Christ. It is a new gospel. The cheeks of the bridegroom are "beds of spices, banks sweetly scented" (Song of Songs 5:13), and the divine action is the gardener who tends them. It is a garden unlike any other, for every one of its flowers is different except for one thing: their eagerness to abandon themselves to the activity of the gardener and let him do what he wishes. They are happy, for their part, to do what is proper to their state. To let God act and obey his demands on us: that is the gospel and the whole scripture and the law.

(8) *This perfect abandonment is as simple as its results are marvelous.*

This, then, is the straight road to holiness and perfection. This is the great, unique secret of self-abandonment, although it is a secret that is no secret and an art without art. As God demands this self-abandonment from us all, he has explained it clearly and made it simple and easy to grasp. Nothing complicated is expected from us when we enter the way of pure faith, and nothing can be clearer and easier to understand. The mystery is only in what God himself does. Look, for example, at the Eucharist. To change the bread into the body of Jesus Christ is so easy that it can be done by anyone, however ignorant he is, provided he is a priest. Yet it is the supreme mystery and one so dark, so hidden and so incomprehensible that the more spiritually enlightened we are the more faith we need to believe it. The way of pure faith is somewhat similar. It enables us to find God at every moment. Can anything be more magnificent, more mysterious, and more blessed? It is both a whole collection of wonders and a source of them which no thoughts, no preaching, no writing can ever exhaust. What has to be done to produce such an amazing effect? Just one thing: let God act and do all he wishes according to our state in life. Nothing in the spiritual life is easier, and it is within everybody's reach. Yet so wonderful and dark is this road that we need great faith to walk along it. Our reason is suspicious and critical. We are expected to believe in matters we have never known or read about. Everything is completely novel. The Jews said the prophets were holy, but Jesus was a sorcerer. If we, like them, are scandalized, how little faith we have! We do not deserve to enjoy the wonders God is eager to work within all faithful souls.

CHAPTER V

ONLY COMPLETE AND TRUE FAITH ENABLES THE SOUL TO ACCEPT WITH JOY EVERYTHING THAT HAPPENS TO IT

(1) *The reproaches and unjustifiable criticisms of people said to be wise and pious.*

Nothing is safer than the way of self-abandonment, nor is anything plainer, easier or more enjoyable and less subject to blunders and errors. God is loved, Christian duties are fulfilled, we frequent the sacraments and perform every one of those outward, visible acts of religion which are binding on everyone. Our superiors are obeyed and our normal duties are fulfilled. We always resist the temptations of the flesh and the devil, for no one is more careful and alert in doing what they have to than those who walk along this way.

Now if this is true, why is it that such people are so often abused? One reason is that when, like many other Christians, they have done all that is demanded by the strictest theologians, they are expected to adopt tiresome practices which the Church does not require, and if they do not they are told they are wrong. But let us look at a Christian who is satisfied by obeying the commandments of God and the Church. He neither meditates nor contemplates, reads no spiritual books, has no interest in any special devotion, and is concerned with business and the other affairs of life in the world. Can he be condemned? Can we even suspect him of being wrong? Of course not. We must admit this. So, if we leave in peace the Christian of whom I have just spoken, it is only fair not to trouble a soul who not only fulfills the precepts at least as well as the average Christian, but also performs both outward and inner acts of piety which the ordinary Christian hardly knows exist and, if he does, is quite indifferent to them.

Prejudice goes so far as to declare that such souls are suffering from delusions because, when they have done all that the Church requires of them, they feel free to surrender themselves without reserve to the hidden, intimate activity of God and to follow the promptings of his grace whenever they have no other essential duties to carry out. In short, they are blamed because they spend that time in loving God which others give to amusement and worldly affairs. Now is not this grossly unfair? This point cannot be too strongly stressed. Let us take someone who lives conventionally and goes to confession once a year. No one talks about him and he is left in peace, except for an occasional suggestion to try to do a little more, but the pressure on him is never great and the suggestion is never made a matter of obligation. But if it should happen that he decides to rise above the mass of conventional Christians, he will be overwhelmed with advice about his spiritual life. If he does not commit himself to follow the established rules of spirituality, he is in trouble. People imagine the worst and mistrust his manner of life. Surely they should realize that these rules, however good and useful, are only the road leading to union with God. Do they want someone who has reached this goal to stay on the road? Yet this is what they ask of a soul which they think is the victim of delusion. But this soul started on this road as so many others have done. It knew and followed faithfully all the accepted practices, but now it would be pointless to try to compel it to remain subject to them. For God, moved by the efforts this soul has made to advance by these methods, comes and takes upon himself to lead it to that blessed union. So since the soul has reached the region where the whole climate is one of self-abandonment and where love enables us to possess God, and since he, who is all goodness, has replaced all these methods and practices by himself, they are no longer of any use to the soul. They are the road by which it once traveled and has now been left behind. If we insist that such a soul should return to these methods, we are asking it to abandon the goal it has reached and return to the road which led it there. If this soul is experienced, such demands

would be a waste of time and trouble, for it will remain quite
unmoved by all turmoil, indifferent to all noise and uproar.
Ignoring them all, it will stay peaceful and unmoved in that
intimate peace where it benefits so greatly by the manifestation of its love. This is the center where it rests; or, if you prefer, it is the straight line drawn by the hand of God and one
which it will always follow. It will walk steadfastly along it
and, from moment to moment, it will be told its duties. As
they appear, they will be fulfilled without any haste or fluster.
In everything else, this soul will preserve a perfect liberty,
always ready to obey the stirrings of grace the moment it becomes aware of them, and to surrender itself to the care of
providence.

God tells the soul that he is its master and he means to
direct it as he wishes, so it must not tolerate any check on its
own freedom or it would be attacking the overriding rights
of its creator. For if it felt itself bound to the rules which
govern those who conduct their lives by them and their own
efforts instead of co-operating with God's grace, it would cut
itself off from a thousand things it needs to fulfill its future
duties. But as people do not know this, they condemn this
attitude for its simplicity, so the souls who condemn no one,
who approve every state of life and know very well how to
assess the various stages of spiritual progress, are yet despised
by those would-be pundits who can never rightly value this
gentle and wholehearted submission to providence.

The worldly-wise have no sympathy with the endless wan-
derings of the Apostles, who could not settle anywhere, and
many ordinary religious people cannot bear the thought of
souls who let all they do depend on providence. But there
are a few who approve of them, and God, who teaches men
by means of their fellow creatures, always ensures that they
come across those who have simply and trustingly abandoned
themselves. These latter need less direction than others, for
they have only reached their present state with the help of
very sound directors, and if they sometimes find that they are
left on their own, it is because providence has removed these
directors, either by death or by sending them to a post a long
distance away. But they remain willing to be directed and
peacefully await the will of God. When they are suffering this

privation, they meet from time to time persons they feel they can trust, although they know nothing about them. This is a sign that God is using these strangers to help them, and the deprived souls ask advice of them and follow it with the greatest docility. But if they do not come across such people, they follow the maxims given them by their first directors, and so they never lack sound direction.

(2) *The apparent uselessness and faults of people chosen by God for the state of abandonment.*

In the eyes of the world, these people are useless nonentities. They can expect neither esteem nor reward. This is not to suggest that people who hold important positions are thereby prevented from attaining the state of self-abandonment; nor, of course, is this state inconsistent with great holiness, which attracts universal veneration. Yet a vastly greater number of souls in this state have their virtue known only to God. Their condition sets them free from nearly every external obligation, and they are not suitable for worldly affairs or for anything demanding thought or steady application. They seem quite useless, weak in mind and body, with no creative power and lacking in all emotion. They involve themselves in nothing, they plan nothing, they foresee nothing and set their hearts on nothing. They are, as it were, quite uncivilized and have none of those qualities which general culture, study and thought give a human being. They are like children before they have been taught how to behave, and we notice their faults which, though no worse than children's, shock us more. God strips them of everything except their innocence so they have nothing but him alone. The world, knowing nothing of this, can judge only by appearances, finds nothing likable or worthwhile about them and so rejects and despises them. They are the laughingstock of everybody. The more closely they are observed, the more they are disliked. No one knows what to make of them. Yet there is an indefinable something which seems to testify in their favor, but people prefer to give way to their spiteful impulses rather than pay attention to this testimony or at least suspend judgment. They keep a sharp watch on all they do, and, just as the Pharisees detested the behavior of Jesus, they are so prejudiced that all they see appears foolish or criminal.

(3) *Interior humiliations.*

These poor souls who are so scorned by others despise themselves just as much. All they do, all they suffer seems as trifling and despicable to them as it does to others. There is nothing impressive about them. Everything is very ordinary. They are spiritually and mentally troubled, and their everyday lives are full of disappointments. They are often unwell and need many attentions and comforts, the very opposite of the austere poverty so much admired in the saints. In them we can see no burning zeal, no achievement of great enterprises, no overwhelming charity and no heroic austerity. Though united to God by faith and love, they find nothing but confusion within themselves. What makes them still more self-contemptuous is when they compare themselves with those who pass for saints, find no difficulty in their spiritual lives in submitting to rules and methods and show nothing out of the way in their characters or actions. They are overwhelmed with shame. Their sorrow and misery at this are responsible for all their sighs and tears. We must remember that Jesus was both God and man. As man he was destroyed, but as God all glory was his. These souls have no part of his glory, but they feel all the annihilating anguish of what seems to be their wretched state. Everyone values them about as much as Herod and his court esteemed Jesus. As far as their senses and mind are concerned, these poor souls are disgusted. Nothing pleases them. They crave for something completely different, but every road which leads to the sanctity they long for is blocked. They must live on this bitter bread of anguish and exist under unrelenting pressure, for they have a conception of sanctity which never ceases to torment them. Their will hungers for it, but they cannot attain it. Why is this? Surely it is to mortify them spiritually so that they can find no pleasure or satisfaction in anything, but must give all their affection to God. He deliberately leads them along this path so that he alone can delight them.

It seems to me that it is obvious from all this that these souls, who have abandoned themselves to God, cannot, as others do, become attached to people or concern themselves with normal aspirations, normal pursuits and activities. Nor can they make plans, look ahead or organize any methodical system for their activities or even for their reading. If they did, it would imply that they were still free to run their lives as they wished, and that would be a denial of their self-abandonment. In that state they surrender to God all their rights over themselves, over their thoughts, their words, their actions and the use they make of every moment. They have only one duty: to keep their gaze fixed on their Master, listen intently to what he wishes and then do it at once. They are exactly like a servant who instantly obeys every order his master gives and never spares a second for his own affairs, which he ignores so that he can serve his master at any moment.

We must not become upset and worried by the humiliations which come from the aspect we present to the world. Let us shelter behind this outer husk and enjoy God, who is all in all to us. Let us benefit by our weaknesses and failures, our fears and doubts; let us draw good from our infirmities, which make us need special food and care, and from the contempt we are shown. Let us find all our happiness in God, who by these means gives himself to us as our only good. He wants the dwelling we offer him to be poverty-stricken and without any of those manifestations of holiness which win such admiration for other souls. He wishes to be our only nourishment and the only one we desire. If we had the virtues of almsgiving, zeal, austerity and poverty, we are so weak that we should take pride in them. Instead, everything is disagreeable, and so God is our sole support and the only means of achieving holiness. The world despises us and leaves us to enjoy our riches in peace. God desires to be the unique cause of all that is holy in us, so all that comes from us is very little. In God's sight there can be nothing great in us—with one exception: our total receptivity to his will. God knows how to make us holy, so let us leave the business to him and think

no more about it. All depends on the vigilant care and action
of providence. We are usually unaware of them and they
often work in ways which are both unexpected and unpleasant to us. Let us tranquilly perform all our little duties and
not look for great ones, for God does not give himself to us
because of our own efforts. We shall become saints through
his grace and by his special providence. He knows to what
eminence he wishes to raise us. Let us leave it to him. Let us
cease hankering after pointless systems of spirituality. Let us
be satisfied to love him ceaselessly and to walk with docility
along the path he has marked out for us, where everything
seems so trivial to us and to the world.

(4)   *The darkness in which these abandoned souls live
and their apparent opposition to the will of God.*

There is nothing more distressing for a soul that wants to
do only the will of God and yet cannot feel certain that it
loves him. Formerly it received spiritual enlightenment which
enabled it to see what the plan was for its perfection, but
now in its present state, it can no longer do so. Perfection is
presented to it contrary to all its preconceived ideas, to all
that it feels and to all that it has learned. It now comes to
the soul in the form of all the afflictions sent by providence,
in the duties of the present moment, in various desires which
have no good about them beyond the fact that they do not
lead to sin. This seems very far from all the sublime and extraordinary glory of holiness. A veiled and hidden God gives
himself and his grace in a strange, unknown manner, for the
soul feels too weak to bear its crosses, distaste for its duties,
and is attracted only to very ordinary spiritual exercises. The
image of sanctity which it has reproaches this soul for its
own mean and despicable nature. It is condemned by all the
books about the lives of saints and can find nothing in its
defense. It beholds a radiant holiness, yet is made wretched
by it for it has not enough strength to reach it and mistakes
this weakness for cowardice instead of an imposition, as it is,
by God. The people it knows who are renowned for their
merits and the elevation of their thoughts regard it with con-

tempt. "What a strange sort of saint!" they say, and the unhappy soul believes them and, ashamed of all the useless efforts it has made to escape from its condition, sinks beneath these reproaches and can make no satisfactory reply either to itself or to others.

In this condition the soul feels as if it were lost without any guide. It no longer has the support of those spiritual meditations which used to strengthen and enlighten it, and it no longer feels the workings of grace. Yet through this loss the soul gains everything. That same grace, adopting, as it were, a different form, gives back to the soul, by the simplicity of its hidden promptings, a hundred times more than it took away.

This is certainly something like a death blow to the soul, for it loses sight of the divine will, which, so to speak, withdraws itself from view and stands behind the soul to push it forward. So it is no longer the clearly defined objective of the soul, but its invisible mainspring. Experience proves that nothing stimulates the desire for union with the divine will so powerfully as this apparent loss. How intense is the soul's grief, and nowhere does it find any consolation.

To snatch God from a heart which longs only for God—this is indeed a mysterious love! And a great one, for it is in this way and no other that absolute faith and firm hope are established in the soul. Then we believe what we cannot see and we hope for what we can only imagine. Oh! how we are brought to perfection by this hidden activity of which we are both the subject and the instrument, though we know nothing of it, for all we do seems to be the result of pure chance and our natural inclinations. Everything humiliates us. When we are actually inspired to speak, we think we are uttering only our all-too-human thoughts. We never know what spirit moves us, we are terrified by the most undoubtedly divine inspiration, and whatever we do or feel fills us with endless contempt for ourselves, as if our whole life were flawed and faulty. We always admire other people and feel vastly inferior to them, and their whole behavior makes us ashamed of ourselves. We mistrust any insight we have, place no reliance on our own thoughts, but pay excessive attention to the most trifling advice from others, if it seems good. God seems to keep us at a distance from all that is virtuous, only to plunge us into a profound humility. We do not think this humility is a virtue, but see it as the judgment of God.

What is really astonishing is that to those who have not been enlightened by God about the true state of affairs, we seem to be obstinate, disobedient, troublesome, contemptuous and angry. We feel this way about ourselves too, and there seems to be no remedy. The harder we try to cure these faults the worse they get, for they are part of God's design and the best means of destroying self-love and preparing us for union with him.

The state of self-abandonment gains its greatest merit from these trials. In performing the duties of the present moment, everything tends to draw us from the path of love and simple obedience. We need great love and heroic courage to hold fast to a straightforward and active faith and to join confidently in the song in which grace also takes part, but sings a different tune in a different key, which convinces us that we are deceived and have gone astray. We hear nothing else, and if we have the courage to ignore the rumbling of the thunder, the lightning flashes and the tumult of the tempest and advance steadily along the way of love and of obedience to the duties and inspirations of every moment, it can be said that we resemble Jesus during his Passion, when our Savior walked firmly along the path of love for his Father and in total submission to his will. It was this love and submission that made him behave in a way which seemed completely in conflict with the majesty of such surpassing holiness as his.

The hearts of Jesus and Mary, in that darkest of nights, let the violence of the storm break over them. Their senses were overwhelmed by a torrent of events which seemed wholly opposed to the designs of God, but, unshaken, they continued along this path of love and obedience. They concentrated on what they themselves had to do and left God to do what he wanted about them. They endured the whole tremendous burden of his action, groaned under its weight, but neither staggered nor paused for a single moment. They believed that all would be well, provided they continued along God's path and left everything else to him.

(5) *The outcome of these trials and the conduct of the soul enduring them.*

In this state of self-abandonment, in this path of simple faith, everything that happens to our soul and body, all that occurs in all the affairs of life, has the aspect of death. This should not surprise us. What do we expect? It is natural to this condition. God has his plans for souls and he carries them out very successfully, though they are well-disguised. Under the name of "disguise" are such things as misfortune, illness and spiritual weakness. But in the hands of God everything flourishes and turns to good. He arranges the accomplishment of his highest designs by means which deeply wound our natural feelings: "We know that by turning everything to their good God co-operates with all those who love him" (Rom. 8:28). He brings life out of the shadow of death, and when, with human weakness, we are afraid, faith, which sees good in all things and knows that all is for the best, remains full of a confident courage. As we know that God's activities include everything, direct everything and do everything—apart from what is sinful—the duty of faith is to adore, love and receive with joy all those activities. Full of joy and confidence, we must ignore the deception of appearances and so enjoy the triumph of faith. In this way, I assure you, you will honor God and treat him as God.

To live by faith is to live joyfully, to live with assurance, untroubled by doubts and with complete confidence in all we have to do and suffer at each moment by the will of God. We must realize that it is in order to stimulate and sustain this faith that God allows the soul to be buffeted and swept away by the raging torrent of so much distress, so many troubles, so much embarrassment and weakness, and so many setbacks. For it is essential to have faith to find God behind all this. The divine life is neither seen nor felt, but there is never a moment when it is not acting in an unknown but very sure manner. It is hidden under such things as death of the body, damnation of the soul, and the general disorder of all earthly affairs. Faith is nourished and strengthened by these happenings. It cuts through them all and takes the hand of God, who keeps it alive through everything except sin. A faithful soul should always advance with confidence, regarding all these things as the disguise God assumes, for his immediate presence would terrify us. But God, who comforts the humble, always gives us, however great our feeling of desolation, an inner assurance that we need be afraid of nothing as long as we allow him to act and abandon ourselves to him. Although we are distressed at the loss of our beloved, we somehow feel that we still possess him, and in spite of all our troubles and disturbance, there is something deep-seated within us which keeps us steadfastly attached to God. "Truly," said Jacob, "God is in this place and I never knew it" (Gen. 28:16). You seek for God, beloved soul, and he is everywhere, everything speaks of him, everything offers him to you, he walks beside you, he surrounds you and is within you. He lives with you and yet you try to find him. You seek your own idea of God, although you have him in his reality. You seek perfection and you meet it in all that happens to you. All you suffer, all you do, all your inclinations are mysteries under which God gives himself to you while you are vainly straining after high-flown fancies. God will never come to dwell with you clothed in these imaginings.

Martha tried to please Jesus by cooking him good food, but Mary was content to receive him and listen to him. Yet he deceived even her, and when, after the Resurrection, she looked for him as she imagined he would be, he appeared to her as a gardener. When the Apostles saw Jesus they thought he was a ghost. God disguises himself so that we may reach that pure faith which enables us to recognize him under any appearance. When we know this secret of his, it is useless for him to assume any disguise, for we say: "See where he stands behind our wall. He looks in at the window, he peers through the lattice" (Song of Songs 2:9). Oh! divine Love, hide yourself, test us, mingle, confuse and snap like threads all our ideas and systems. Let us stumble and find neither roads nor paths in the darkness. Formerly we found you in the peace of solitude, in prayer, in various religious exercises, in suffering, in helping our neighbors, in turning away from social and business affairs. We have done all we can to please you, but now we can no longer find you in these things as once we did. May our failure compel us to find you in yourself and then in all things and everywhere. How mistaken we are not to see you in everything that is good and in every creature. Why should we seek you in any other way than that by which you wish to give yourself, under any other forms than those you have chosen for your sacrament? The less convincing they seem, the more merit there is in our obedience and faith.

You make a root below the soil flourish and you can make fruitful the darkness in which you keep me. So my soul, like a tiny root, will stay hidden in you and your power will make it send forth branches, leaves, blossoms and fruit which, though invisible to you, will nourish and delight the souls of others. When they come to rest and refresh themselves in your shade, give them the fruit they want, not what you think they should have. May all that is grafted on you by grace take and ultimately produce its own individual fruit. Give all you have to all who come, but you yourself continue in your state of self-abandonment and indifference. Stay, little silkworm, in the dark and narrow cell of your comfortless cocoon until the warmth of grace enables you to grow and break out. Eat then every leaf grace offers you, and in this activity do not look back at the peace you have lost. The moment God's will tells you to stop, do so. You will experience alternating spells of rest and activity and changes in yourself which you cannot understand. You will lose all interest in all the old spiritual exercises. You will die and be resurrected and assume the apparel that God has designed for you, so spin away in secret, working away at what you can neither see nor feel. Your whole being will be perturbed, you will condemn yourself for being in a fret, and you will secretly envy your companions still lying as if dead because they have not yet arrived where you are. You continue to admire them although you have left them behind. But continue to spin a silk in which princes of the Church and of the world, and indeed a multitude of souls, will glory to be arrayed. And after that, what will happen to you, little silkworms? How will you emerge? What a miracle of grace it is that souls are molded so differently! Who can possibly know where grace will lead them? And who could guess what nature does with a silkworm if he had not seen it? All it needs is leaves, and nature does the rest.

Thus, beloved souls, you cannot know from where you came nor where you are going; nor can you know from what idea of God you have been produced nor to what end it is leading you. For you there remains only a passive self-abandonment, carrying on without thinking and concerned with no models or examples or any particular mode of spirituality. You must act when it is time for action and stop when it is time to stop. In this self-abandonment you read or put books aside, talk to people or keep silent, write or drop your pen, and never know what will follow. Finally, after several transformations, the formed and finished soul, now endowed with wings, flies up to heaven, but leaves on earth a fertile seed to work in other souls.

CHAPTER VI

ALL WILL BE WELL IF WE ABANDON OURSELVES TO GOD

(1) *God truly helps us however much we may feel we have lost his support.*

There is a kind of holiness in which all the messages from God are bright and clear, but there is also that state of utterly quiescent faith in which all that God tells us is wrapped in the impenetrable darkness which veils his throne, and all we feel is confused and shadowy. In this condition, we are often afraid, like the prophet, of running smack into a rock as we advance through this darkness. We should have no fear. We are on the right path and led by God. There is nothing safer and less likely to lead us astray than the darkness of faith. Yet we want to know which way must we go amidst this darkness? Wherever we wish. It does not matter. We cannot get lost when there is no road to be found. Nor can we head for any particular destination, for we can see nothing at all. We say: "I am terrified of everything. It seems as if, at any minute, I might fall headlong over a precipice. I know perfectly well that I am obeying the demands of self-abandonment, but it seems to me that whatever I do is far from virtuous. I hear all the virtues complaining that I am deserting them, and the more deeply I am moved by these complaints the further away does the hidden power which controls me seem to drive me. I love virtue but yield to this power, and though I cannot perceive that it is a trustworthy guide, I cannot stop myself believing that it is."

The spirit seeks the light, but the heart longs for the dark. The words of every intellectual person fascinate my mind, but my heart cares only for incomprehensible talks and lectures. The whole of my being is so immersed in faith that I love and appreciate those principles, those truths and those methods in which I can see no point and where, in contemplating them, my mind becomes confused and falters. Yet I still feel certain, though I don't know why, that everything is all right, not through any evidence but because faith convinces me. For it is impossible for God to guide a soul without giving it the certainty that it is on the right path, a conviction which is greater the less it is perceived, and one which conquers all fear and all the reasoning of the mind. It is in vain that the intellect protests and struggles to find a better way. The bride senses the presence of the bridegroom without feeling him, for when she tries to touch him he disappears. "His right arm embraces her" (Song of Songs 2:6) and she prefers to abandon herself to his guidance, even though it seems without rhyme or reason, rather than try to reassure herself by struggling along the beaten paths of virtue. So come, my soul, come and let us go to God by self-abandonment. Let us acknowledge that we are incapable of becoming holy by our own efforts, and put our trust in God, who would not have taken away our ability to walk unless he was to carry us in his arms. What, Lord, is the use to us of being able to see, to feel and to understand, as we are not making our journey on foot but are being carried in your arms? Our trust and our faith will deepen the darker it grows; and as we pass great gorges and jagged peaks and across vast deserts, and become terrified by persecution, famine and drought and visions of hell and purgatory, we have only to glance at you to feel safe amidst the greatest peril. We shall forget the roads and what they are like, forget ourselves and abandon ourselves entirely to the wisdom, the goodness and the power of our guide, and remember only to love you and avoid the slightest sin and fulfill all our obligations. This, my Beloved, is all your children have to do. You take charge of everything else. And the more terrible this "everything" is, the more surely do they experience your presence. They think only of loving you and fulfill their little duties like a child playing in his mother's lap as if there were nothing in the world but his mother and his toys. The soul must move beyond these shadows. The night is not the time for action but for rest. The light of reason can only deepen the darkness of faith. The only rays which can pierce it must come from the same source as the darkness—from above. When, in this darkness, God communicates with the soul he comes as life, but is no longer visible as the way and the truth (John 14:6). During this darkness the bride seeks the bridegroom (Song of Songs 3:1), but he stays behind her, holds her in his hands and pushes her ahead of him. No longer is he the object on which our ideas are fixed, but is the principle and source of all things. No matter what troubles, unhappiness, worries, upsets, doubts and needs harass souls who have lost all confidence in their own powers, they can all be overcome by the marvelous hidden and unknown power of the divine action. The more perplexing the situation, the more we can hope for a happy solution. The heart says: "All will be well. God has the matter in hand. We need fear nothing." Our very fear and sense of desolation are verses in this hymn of darkness. We delight in singing every syllable of them, knowing that all ends with the "Glory be to the Father." So we follow our wandering paths, and the very darkness acts as our guide and our doubts serve to reassure us. The more puzzled Isaac was at not finding a lamb for the sacrifice, the more confidently did Abraham leave all to providence (Gen. 22:7–8).

(2) *The afflictions which souls endure are loving deceptions of God which will one day fill them with great joy.*

Souls who walk in light sing the hymns of light; those who walk in the shadows chant the hymns of darkness. Each must be allowed to sing through to the end the words and melody which God has given him. Nothing must be changed in what he has composed. Every drop of distress, bitter as gall though it may be, must be allowed to flow, no matter what its effect on us. It was the same for Jeremiah and Ezekiel, whose every utterance was broken by sighs and tears. They found consolation only in continuing their laments. Had their tears been halted, we should have lost the loveliest passages in Scripture. The spirit which makes us suffer is the only one which can comfort us. These different waters flow from the same source. If God seems angry, we tremble; if he threatens us, we are terrified. But we can only let the divine project develop, for within itself it contains both the disease and its cure. So, beloved souls, weep and tremble. Remain in torment. Make no attempt to escape from these divinely inspired terrors. Receive in the depths of your hearts the little streams which flow from the sea of sorrow which filled the most holy soul of Jesus. Keep advancing and let your tears flow under the influence of grace. This same influence will finally dry your eyes. The clouds will drift away, the sun will shine again, spring will adorn you with its flowers, and then you will see, because of your abandonment, the full extent of what the divine action is accomplishing. It is really useless to become agitated, for all that happens to us is like a dream. Shadowy images come and go, and dreams, passing through our sleeping mind, give us both pain and pleasure. Our soul is the plaything of these phantoms, but when we awaken we know at once that they have not really affected us. Their impression quickly fades and our waking life pays no heed to the perils or delights of sleep.

Now, Lord, can I not say that you carry all your sleeping children during the night of faith? And that you allow to stream through their souls an infinite number of holy and mysterious ideas? During this night and sleep of faith they cause great terror and anguish, which, when the day of glory dawns, you will transform into real and solid joy.

Once these souls are fully awake, have come to and are at last able to use their own judgment, they will never tire of admiring the adroitness, the subtlety, the finesse and the loving deceptions of the bridegroom. And they will understand that they can never comprehend his methods, never solve his puzzles, never penetrate his disguises, nor know any comfort when he wishes to cause them terror and alarm. It is at an awakening such as this that Jeremiah and David realized that all which filled them with profound distress gave great joy to God and his angels. Do not awaken the bride. Leave her to sigh and tremble and pursue the bridegroom. It is true that he disguises himself to deceive her. But let her sleep on (Song of Songs 3:5). Her dreams and fears are born only of sleep and the night. The bridegroom will be active within this beloved soul and do to it what only he can accomplish. When the hour comes, he will awaken it. Joseph made Benjamin weep, and his servants did not reveal his secret. Joseph deceived him completely, and Benjamin and his brothers felt a bitter sorrow and saw no hope anywhere. Yet when he revealed who he was, all was put right, and they admired his wisdom in producing the greatest joy they had ever known from so much apparent misery and despair.

(3) *The more God seems to take from the abandoned soul, the more he is really giving it.*

Let us gain greater knowledge of the divine activity. When God takes from us the things we can see and understand, he always returns them under another form. He never lets us want. It is as if a man had supported a friend openly and generously and then, for the friend's own good, suddenly pretended he could not provide for him, yet continued to furnish secretly all he needed. Now, this friend, knowing nothing of this mysterious stratagem of love, would feel upset and brood unhappily on the behavior of his former benefactor. But as soon as he began to understand what was really happening, God only knows all the feelings of joy, love, gratitude, embarrassment and wonder that filled his soul! And how much more affection will he have for his benefactor! And think how this trial will strengthen his feeling for his friend and brace him against any similar shocks! It is easy to draw a lesson from all this: where God is concerned, the more we seem to lose, the more we gain; the more he strips us of natural things, the more he showers us with supernatural gifts. We certainly loved him a little for these gifts, but when we could no longer be aware of them we loved him for himself alone. He appears to take away these gifts so that he can give them the greatest gift of all, the one that is most precious because it embraces within itself all the others. Any soul which has, once and for all, completely submitted itself to God, should always interpret everything favorably: the loss of the most able spiritual directors and the mistrust it feels for those who push themselves forward as replacements.

For, usually, those would-be guides who chase after souls should quite rightly be mistrusted. Those genuinely moved by the spirit of God have not, as a rule, so much eagerness and complacency. They prefer to wait until they are summoned, and even then they come forward rather hesitantly. So let the self-abandoned soul have no fear when passing through these trials. As long as it co-operates with God's action, that action will achieve wonders within it, in spite of every obstacle.

God and the soul work together and all goes well when the soul is healthy, for though the success of God's action depends, of course, on him, it can be spoiled if the soul proves unfaithful. God's achievement is like the front of a lovely tapestry. The worker employed on such a tapestry sees only the back as he adds stitch after stitch with his needle, yet all these stitches are slowly creating a magnificent picture which appears in all its glory only when every stitch is done and it is viewed from the right side. But all this beauty cannot be seen as it is being created. It is the same with the self-abandoned soul. It sees only God and its duty. To fulfill this duty moment by moment consists in adding tiny stitches to the work; yet it is by these stitches that God accomplishes those marvels of which we sometimes catch a glimpse now, but which will not be truly known until the great day of eternity. How good and wise are the ways of God! All that is sublime and exalted, great and admirable in the task of achieving holiness and perfection, he has kept for his own power; but everything that is small, simple and easy he leaves us to tackle with the help of grace. So there is not a single person who cannot easily reach the highest degree of perfection by performing every duty, no matter how commonplace, with eager love.

(4)   *God seems to blind the abandoned soul, but, in fact, he is guiding it very safely.*

These words of St. John apply especially to the souls wholly abandoned to God: "You have been anointed by the Holy One and have all received the knowledge" (I John 2:20).

For these souls, their hearts tell them what God desires. They have only to listen to the promptings of their hearts to interpret his will in the existing circumstances. God's plans, disguised as they are, reveal themselves to us through our intuition rather than through our reason. They disclose themselves in various ways: by chance or by what seems to be a compulsive thrust which allows no choice of action, by a sudden impulse, by some supernatural rapture, or very often by something which attracts or repels us. Now, if we judge all this superficially, it certainly seems that it is not very sensible to leave so important an affair to such uncertainty. Judging by ordinary standards, there is no order and indeed no sense, in this way of going on. Nevertheless, to obey this apparent disorder is to have reached the summit of virtue, and it is one we do not reach without long years of effort. This virtue is pure, unadulterated virtue. It is, quite simply, perfection. When we reach it, we are like a musician who, apart from having played all his life, has a complete knowledge of all the theory and techniques of music. All he plays, without even thinking about it, is perfect, and, if he writes music, all his compositions will be found to square with every rule governing the writing of music. And why? Because he does not set himself to obey the rules which, when interpreted too literally, fetter genius; he writes without constraint and his impromptu pieces are very rightly thought to be masterpieces. In the same way, the soul which has for a very long time studied and worked to achieve perfection and used every method to co-operate with grace gradually falls into the habit of acting always by an instinctive following of God's wishes. Such a soul realizes that it can do nothing better than deal with whatever first crops up without all the careful thought it formerly used to need. It must act at random, following those promptings of grace which cannot lead it astray. And what grace does is nothing short of marvelous to those who observe it with clear eyes and intelligent minds. There are no rules, yet there is perfect organization; no proper arrangements, yet all is well ordered; no serious thinking, yet profound conclusions; no effort, yet everything done well; no foresight, yet swift adaptation to every new happening.

The reading of books of spirituality often, by God's direction, take on meanings that their authors never dreamt of. For God uses the words and actions of others to disclose truths which would otherwise have been hidden, and if he wishes to enlighten us in this way, we self-abandoned ones must make full use of it, being well aware that anything inspired by God is far more effective than one would imagine from looking at it from the purely human viewpoint.

It is of the essence of the state of self-abandonment that, although the soul thus abandoned always leads a secret life, it yet receives from God most extraordinary gifts by means of the most ordinary things and by events which seem quite natural and mere casual happenings, through occurrences which appear to be a normal part of human life. For instance, the simplest sermons, the most ordinary conversations and the most trivial books can become, through God's will, sources of knowledge and wisdom. This is why self-abandoned souls always carefully gather up the crumbs which the proud tread underfoot, for everything is precious to them and there is nothing which does not enrich them. They are completely indifferent to everything, yet neglect nothing, for they respect all things and extract from them all that is useful.

As God is in all things, the use we make of them is not actually the use of creatures but the delight of obeying his will expressed through so many diverse channels. Now, these channels have no power in themselves to help us to holiness, but as instruments of the divine will they can transmit his grace and often do so to simple souls by ways and means which seem opposed to the intended end. To God, mud is as transparent as the air, and the instrument he uses is always unique for its purpose, for to him all things are alike. If our faith is strong we shall be confident that we lack nothing and shall never complain that we have not the means which might be useful for our advancement. For the Workman, who uses these means, ensures that we have all we need. His most holy will gives us everything.

(5) *Although the abandoned soul seems incapable of defending itself, God himself protects it with all his powers.*

The unique and absolutely certain action of God is always applied to a submissive soul at exactly the right time, and this soul at once reacts as it should. It accepts all that has happened, all that is happening, and co-operates with everything except with what is sinful. There are times when the soul acts consciously and at times quite unknowingly, being instinctively moved to say, to do or to ignore certain things without having any apparent reason for such behavior. Often the motive force is something quite natural, and the simple soul sees nothing mysterious about it and acts through pure chance, necessity or convenience. Neither this soul nor any other sees anything strange about it. Yet it is God, through the intellect, the wisdom or the advice of friends, who is using these ordinary means. He makes them his own instruments and employs them in such a way that no plans of any enemies directed against his chosen souls can possibly succeed. To deal with a simple soul is to deal with God. What can be done against the unfathomable ways of the Almighty? God takes over the cause of the simple soul, and then it has nothing to worry about, no intrigues to fear, no need to keep a careful watch on other people. It is carefree and rests in the bridegroom's arms safe and at peace. God frees us from all the ignoble and devious tricks which seem necessary to human prudence. Such tricks suited Herod and the Pharisees, but all the Magi had to do was follow their star in peace, and the Child had only to rest in his mother's arms. His enemies benefited rather than harmed him, and the more they tried to thwart and trap him, the more freely and calmly did he act. He never humored them nor did he ever flatter them to escape their blows, their envy and their suspicion. Their persecution was necessary for him. That is how Jesus Christ lived in Judea, and this is how he continues to live in simple souls. With them he is generous and gentle, unreserved and friendly. He neither fears nor needs anyone, for he sees all creatures in his Father's hands and knows they are bound to serve him. Some give this service by their evil passions, some by their holy deeds, others by their glad obedience. It is all wonderfully arranged: nothing is lacking, nor is there too much of anything. There is just what there should be of both good and evil. At every moment God's will produces what is needful for the task in hand, and the simple soul, instructed by faith, finds everything as it should be and wants neither more nor less than what it has. It never ceases to praise the divine hand for the way it smooths the path ahead. It receives both friends and enemies with the same kindness, just as Jesus treated everyone as God's agent. We have need of no one, yet we need everybody. God wills that everything and everyone are necessary and we must accept them from him just as they are, receiving them kindly and humbly. We must be simple with the simple and kind with the rude and coarse. This is what St. Paul taught. "For the weak I made myself weak. I made myself all things to all men in order to save some at any cost" (I Cor. 9:22). And Jesus Christ practiced it perfectly.

Only grace can give a soul that supernatural quality which enables it to show such a detailed and suitable understanding of the nature of each person. It is something never learned from books. There is something truly visionary about it which comes from a special revelation and the teaching of the Holy Spirit. The soul must have reached the highest state of self-abandonment before it can understand it, and must be utterly detached from every project and from any affair or concern, no matter how holy they may be. The soul must concentrate on the supreme business of life: submission to God's will so that it can give itself up to fulfilling the obligations of its circumstances. Let us leave the Holy Spirit to act upon it without thinking of what he is doing and being well content to know nothing about it, confident that all that happens in the world is only for the benefit of souls obedient to God's will.

(6)   *An abandoned soul is not afraid of its enemies, but finds them useful allies.*

I am more afraid of what I and my friends do than of anything done by my enemies. There is nothing more prudent than to offer no resistance to one's enemies and face them in simple self-abandonment. This is to run before the wind and stay at peace. Simplicity is always victorious when faced with worldly wisdom and easily avoids all its tricks without understanding them or even being conscious of them. God makes the soul take such suitable measures that they completely confound those who seek to trap it. It benefits by all their efforts, and what is meant to degrade it only increases its virtue. Their stratagems bring it into its harbor like galley slaves rowing all out. All obstacles help it so much that, by giving its enemies a free hand, it gets from them such ample and continuous advantages that it must beware that it does not join in and take part in a work which God wishes to do himself with these enemies as his agent. All the soul has to do is observe peacefully the activities of God and, in all simplicity, follow those inspirations which come from the Holy Spirit, who always knows the true significance of everything and directs the soul, without its knowledge, so suitably that all who are its enemies are inevitably destroyed.

(7)   *An abandoned soul never need try to justify itself by word or deed. God does that.*

The huge, unyielding rock that shelters the soul from all storms is the divine will, which is always there, though hidden beneath the veil of trials and the most commonplace actions. Deep within those shadows is the hand of God to support and carry us to complete self-abandonment. And when a soul has arrived at this sublime state it need fear nothing which is said against it, for there is no longer anything for it to say or do in self-defense. Since it is the work of God, we must not try to justify it. Its effects and its consequences will

vindicate it enough. There is nothing to be done but let them
unfold. If we no longer rely on our own ideas, we must not
try to defend ourselves with words, for words can only express our ideas. So, no ideas, no words. What use would they
be? To give reasons for our behavior? But we do not know
these reasons, for they are hidden in the source of our actions,
and from that source we have received only influences we can
neither describe nor understand. So we must let the consequences justify themselves. Every link in this divine chain is
unbreakable, and the meaning of what has happened earlier
is seen in the consequences which follow. The soul no longer
lives in a world of thoughts, of imagination, of endless words.
Now these no longer occupy it; neither do they nourish or
sustain it. It no longer sees where it is going or where it will
go. It relies no longer on its own ideas to help it to bear the
weariness and difficulties of the journey. It carries on with a
profound conviction of its own weakness. But with each step
the road widens and, having started, the soul advances along
it without hesitation. It is innocent, simple and faithful and
follows the straight path of God's commandments, relying on
him, whom it meets continually along this path.

(8) *An abandoned soul is preserved by God by means
which seem more likely to destroy it.*

There is a time when God desires to animate the whole of
the soul and bring it to perfection secretly and by unknown
ways. It is then that a soul's own ideas, intuitions, work, in-
vestigations and inferences become sources of delusion. After
several experiences of the folly into which it is led by its efforts to guide itself, the soul recognizes how helpless it is and
discovers that God has so hidden and entangled all the channels through which his love flows that it has to find life in
God himself. So, convinced of its own nothingness and certain, too, that all it can derive from itself is harmful, it
abandons itself to God so that it can have only him and receive all things through him. It is then that God becomes the
source of its life, not because of anything it has thought
about, or through any illumination, for all this is no longer

anything but a source of illusion. The soul's new attitude comes about through the reality and the efforts of God's grace, hidden and disguised though it is. The soul knows nothing of God's operations, yet it receives from them all their efficacy through countless events which it believes will destroy it. There is nothing we can do about this ignorance. We must just put up with it. But it is within this ignorance that God gives himself and all other things. The soul is blind or like a sick person who finds all his medicines unpleasant but never realizes the good they are doing him. He often thinks they will kill him. And the weakness and various relapses which follow his taking of them seem to justify his fears. But, although he appears to be near death, he regains his health because he takes the medicine on his doctor's word.

Of course, there are really ill people who have to stay in bed and be treated by their doctors, but the debility and weakness which self-abandoned souls experience are quite different. They are not real illnesses and they should ignore them. It is God who makes them feel like this, and he does it so that they are thrown back on their faith and abandon themselves to him completely. It is the only remedy. These souls should carry on cheerfully along the road, ignoring all the suffering that God sends them and using their bodies like a hired horse which is driven until it collapses. This is far better than pampering ourselves and weakening our spiritual energy. This energy can surprisingly fortify a feeble body, and a single year spent with nobility and generosity is worth more than a hundred passed in worrying about trifles. We should try always to carry ourselves with the air of a child blessed by God's grace and his good will. What on earth have we to fear if we follow him? As his children, led and upheld by him, our whole attitude should be one of fearlessness. The terrors we meet on our journey are really nothing. They are sent only so that our lives may be made more splendid by our overcoming them. God involves us in every kind of trouble, and ordinary human common sense, seeing no way out of it, realizes all its weakness and shortcomings and feels completely baffled. It is at this moment that God appears in all his glory to those who belong wholly to him and disentangles them from all their troubles far more easily than novelists, working away in the peace of their rooms, extricate their heroes from all their dangers and bring them to a happy and successful end. With far greater skill and most happily does God lead them through deadly perils, monstrous happenings, through hell itself and its demons and all their snares. He sweeps these souls up to heaven and transforms them into the heroes of stories far stranger and more lovely than any invented by the stunted imaginings of men. So, my soul, plunge ahead, sweeping through all the monster-plagued dangers ahead, knowing that you are guided and sustained by the mighty, yet invisible, hand of God. Let us carry on to the end without the slightest tremor of fear, but full of peace and joy, with everything that befalls us becoming the occasion for fresh triumphs. We march under God's banner to fight and to conquer: "He went from victory to victory" (Rev. 6:2). Every step we take under his command is a victory. God has his pen and an open book before him, and in this book he writes a blessed story which will end only when the world ends, for it is an account of God's dealings with men and women. If we want to have a place in this story, we must ensure that we link all we do and suffer with God's will. I most solemnly assure you that all your actions and sufferings are not meant to destroy you. They serve to help to fill this holy book of God, which grows every day.

(9)   *The love God showers on us replaces everything for us if we accept it.*

God takes away everything from us if we give ourselves entirely to him, but he gives us something else far better. He deprives us of strength, wisdom and everything that seems to make life worthwhile. But then he gives us his love. And this love burns within us like a supernatural fire. In the world of nature all things have what they need. Every flower has its particular charm, every animal has the right instincts, and, indeed, all creatures have their own special fitness for their existence. And so it is in the world of grace: each one of us has a special grace, and this is a reward for all of us who cheerfully accept the state in which God has placed us. A soul comes under the influence of God from the moment it turns toward him, and this influence fluctuates according to the extent of the soul's abandonment. The whole business of self-abandonment is only the business of loving, and love achieves everything. Nothing can be denied it. How can our love possibly be rejected? How can the love of God refuse anything to a soul whose every act it controls? And how can a soul which lives for him and him alone refuse him anything? What love desires, love cannot refuse, nor can it want anything that love rejects. God troubles about nothing but our good will. He is quite unconcerned about any other of our qualities or lack of them. All he wants from us is an honest, straightforward, simple, submissive and loyal heart. When he finds such a heart, he takes possession of it, controls all its responses, and so uses it that it finds in everything, no matter what, something which is invaluable in its progress to holiness. There are, it is true, elements which might pierce a soul and destroy it, but a soul charged with good will can and does defy such irruptions. And if such a soul finds itself on the edge of a precipice, God will snatch it to safety, and, were it to fall, he would seize it and save it. For, after all, such faults are mere human frailty and are hardly noticed. Besides, God's love can allow the soul to benefit from them. And by subtle and almost imperceptible promptings it persuades the soul to say and do the right thing according to the circumstances in which it finds itself. These promptings are flashes of light from the divine intelligence—a light which illumines every step taken by the soul and so prevents them from going astray, as they so easily might because of their simplicity. Suppose these souls make arrangements which could harm them —well, it doesn't matter. Providence will see to it that they come out of it unscathed. Time and time again people plot against them, but providence comes to their aid, slashes through all the snares and deals with the plotters so that they fall into the traps they have so carefully devised. Under the direction of God these souls seem to do foolish things—but it isn't so. For these things end up by setting them free from all the troubles their enemies had planned for them.

What splendor there is in this exchange of good will between God and man! What good sense there is in genuine simplicity! What virtue in its innocent freedom, what secrets in its uprightness! Look at the young lad Tobias. He is hardly more than a child, yet the great archangel Raphael is at his side, and with such a guide he fears nothing and has all he needs. Even the very monsters who attack him provide him with food and help for his illness. The one which rushes to attack him makes a good meal for him. He concerns himself with nothing but parties and wedding feasts—for that is the decree of providence. There are plenty of other affairs needing his attention, but God has decided that he must attend to these festivities. Never have things gone so well for him: all is blessed and prosperous. Yet his mother weeps bitterly, believing that she will never see him again, but his father's faith never falters, and their son comes safely home and shares their joy. For those who abandon themselves to it, God's love contains every good thing, and if you long for it with all your heart and soul it will be yours. All God asks for is love, and if you search for this kingdom where God alone rules, you can be quite sure you will find it. For if your heart is completely devoted to God, your heart itself is this treasure, this very kingdom which you desire so ardently. The moment we long for God and to obey his will, we enjoy him and all his gifts, and the fullness of our enjoyment exactly matches the extent of our desire for him. To love God is to want to love him in all sincerity, and it is because we love him that we want to serve him as instruments through which he acts both through and in us. The activity of God is not related to any shrewdness shown by a simple and holy soul, but to its loving desires. Nor is God concerned about the plans of this soul, its ideas and the projects it has in mind, for it can easily be wrong about them all, but its uprightness and good intentions can never lead it astray. Once God sees these good intentions, he ignores everything else and regards as having been done what would most certainly be done if the soul's good will were inspired by sounder reasons.

So good will need fear nothing. Should it fall, it stumbles under the protection of that almighty hand which never fails to guide and support it whenever it goes astray. This is the hand which directs it toward its goal if it turns aside, and sets it again on the right path if it leaves it. It helps the soul when it falls into error because of its false judgment and makes it realize how it should mistrust its natural instincts and abandon itself absolutely to the infallible guidance of God. All the mistakes to which even the best of souls are liable cannot harm the self-abandoned, and never does it find itself caught off its guard, for "everything is turned to its good" (Rom. 8:28).

(10) *When the soul has embraced abandonment it receives more insight and strength, by its submission to God's will, than do all those who defy it because of their pride.*

What use to us is the most profound insight and even revelations coming direct from God, if we do not love his will? When God disclosed to Lucifer the mystery of the Incarnation, jealousy consumed him. Yet a simple soul enlightened only by faith never tires of admiring, praising and loving every manifestation of God's will. It finds it shown not only in saints but even in complete chaos and disorder. One grain of pure faith gives more true enlightenment to a simple soul than Lucifer ever gained by his vastly superior intelligence. A simple soul, faithfully fulfilling its duties, contentedly obedient to the suggestions of grace and being gentle and humble to everyone, possesses knowledge worth more than the most profound intellectual penetration of the unknown. If only we could see the divine activity in all the pride and savagery of human activity, we should always behave toward our fellow creatures with kindness and respect. For their turbulence would never affect us. We must never sever our union with the activity of God which is incorporated in them and which they will reveal to us if we stay gentle and humble. We must take no notice of the path they tread, but advance steadfastly along our own. By such gentle resolutions, great cedars are broken and mountains moved. For who can resist the strength of a faithful, gentle and humble soul? These qualities are all the weapons we need to overcome all our enemies. Jesus Christ has placed them in our hands so we can defend ourselves. Once we know how to use them, we need fear nothing. We must not be cowardly, but act with a noble courage, and then we shall be able to use these God-given weapons.

Who is Lucifer? He is a radiant angel and the most en-lightened of all, but an angel hostile to God and his designs. The mystery of sin is merely the result of this hostility, which manifests itself in every possible way. Lucifer does all he can to ensure that all that God has made and governs is over-thrown. Wherever he gets a foothold, the work of God is defaced. The more knowledge and intelligence a person has, the more misgivings we should have about him unless he has not that basic piety which consists in being happy to serve God and do all he wants. A well-disposed heart unites us with God's will. Without it, we behave according to our natural impulses and usually fight against the divine plans. God, strictly speaking, uses only the humble as his instruments. Yet, to fulfill his designs, he makes use of those proud folk who defy him as his slaves. Whenever I come across a soul who thinks only of God and his will, I pay no attention to any other qualities it may lack, but declare: "This is a soul with a genius for serving God." The Blessed Virgin and St. Joseph were like this. A host of other talents without this surpassing virtue terrify me, and I suspect the activity of Lucifer. I stay on my guard and brace myself in opposition to all this bril-liancy, which seems to me to be no more than a bit of fragile glass.

(11) *To the abandoned soul God is visible even in the proud souls who oppose him. Every creature, whether good or evil, reveals God to him.*

The whole principle on which the simple soul bases its life is to do God's will, and he respects its working even in the wicked deeds which the arrogant man commits to affront it. Such a man despises a humble soul, in whose eyes he is a mere cipher, for it sees only God in his person and his deeds. The man of pride often imagines that the unassuming mod-esty of the simple soul is a sign that it fears him, although it is merely the sign of the loving fear of God and his will, as shown to it by this haughty fellow. No, poor fool, the simple soul has no fear of you. You fill it with pity. It is answering God when you think it is talking to you. It knows it is dealing with God and considers you only as one of his slaves or rather as a shadow which disguises him. The haughtier the tone you take, the more softly does it answer you, and when you think to take it by surprise, you are the one who will be startled. For it, all your cheating and violence come as favors from heaven. A proud soul is a riddle which a simple soul enlightened by faith solves very easily.

The realization that God is active in all that happens at every moment is the deepest knowledge we can have in this life of the things of God. It is a continuous revelation, an endlessly renewed traffic with God; the bridegroom is enjoyed without any stealth or secrecy, not in the wine cellar or the vineyard but openly and freely and fearing no one. It is peace, joy, love and a feeling of being at ease with God who is seen and known—or, rather, believed—to be present and always active in the most faultless way in every happening. It is a foretaste of paradise, which is, in this life, only sensed imperfectly through a veil of shadows, but when it comes to the moment of our death, the Holy Spirit, who secretly moves all the pieces on the board of life by his continual and fruitful activity, will say: "Let there be light." Then we shall behold all the riches which faith alone knew were hidden in those depths of peace and contentment with God, who is with us all the time and by our side in all we do and suffer.

When God gives himself thus, the commonplace becomes extraordinary, and so nothing appears to be out of the way. The path along which we go is itself so extraordinary that there is no need to ornament it with extraneous wonders. It is a miracle and a constant delight, yet, in itself, has nothing about it to dazzle our senses, but it does turn all the ordinary affairs of life into things which are rare and wonderful.

(12) *To all his faithful souls, God promises a glorious victory over the powers of the world and of hell.*

God's activity in the world is hidden under an apparent weakness to increase the merits of souls who remain faithful to it, but, in spite of this, its triumph is certain.

Since the world began, its history is nothing but the account of the campaign waged by the powers of the world and the princes of hell against the humble souls who love God. It is a conflict in which all the odds seem to favor pride, yet humility always wins. The image of this world is shown to us as a statue of gold, silver, bronze, iron and earthenware. This mystery of evil, which Nebuchadnezzar saw in a dream (Dan. 2:24), is nothing but a jumble of all the physical and spiritual activities of the children of darkness, together with the beast coming out of the abyss to war against the interior and spiritual life of man. It is a war that has been going on since time began, and everything that happens in the contemporary world is the continuation of this war (Rev. 13:1 *et seq*). Monster follows monster and the abyss engulfs them and spews them forth again amidst incessant clouds of smoke. The war which broke out in heaven between St. Michael and Lucifer is still being fought. The heart of this proud and jealous angel is a bottomless pit from which all wickedness comes. He began civil war between the angels of heaven, and since the creation of the world his sole aim has been to enroll regiments of scoundrels, wicked men, to fill the ranks of those he has swallowed up. Lucifer is the chief of those who defy God. This mystery of evil turns upside down the good order of God, replacing it with the order—or, rather, the disorder—of the devil.

This disorder is a curious thing, because though superficially attractive, it hides evils which are incurable and infinite. Every wicked man since Cain, up until those who now consume the world, have outwardly appeared to be great and powerful princes. They have astonished the world and men have bowed down before them. But the face they present to the world is false. For they are beasts who have filed out from the pit to overthrow the order of God. But this order—another mystery—has never failed to produce great and powerful men who have slain these monsters, and as new ones are vomited forth from hell, heaven has created new heroes to destroy them. All ancient history, both sacred and profane, is only the record of this conflict. The order established by God has always conquered, and those who have fought with him enjoy eternal happiness. Deserters from his ranks receive eternal death as their reward.

The wicked man is always certain that he is invincible. But, O God, how can we withstand you? If one solitary soul has all the powers of hell and the world against it, it need fear nothing if it has abandoned itself to the order of God.

This monstrous image of wickedness and power, with its head of gold and its body of silver, bronze and iron, is only a phantom of glittering dust. A tiny pebble shatters it and the winds sweep it away (Dan. 2:34).

How wonderfully has the Holy Spirit moved through all the centuries of created time! So many revolutions and uprisings, so many great and good men moving like the stars above us, so many wonderful happenings—yet it is all like Nebuchadnezzar's dream, forgotten when he awakens, no matter how terrible the impression it made.

All these monsters come into the world only to stimulate the courage of the children of God, and when they have finished their training, God allows them to slay the monster. Heaven receives the victors and hell engulfs the vanquished. A new monster appears and God summons fresh warriors into the arena. Our life here is a spectacle which makes heaven rejoice, rears up saints and confounds hell. And so all that opposes the rule of God only succeeds in making it more worthy of being adored. All the enemies of justice become its slaves, and God builds the heavenly Jerusalem with the fragments of Babylon the destroyed.

IMAGE STUDY GUIDE

Abandonment to Divine Providence
by Jean-Pierre de Caussade

TRANSLATED AND INTRODUCED
BY JOHN BEEVERS

OVERVIEW

"Caussade was a very simple man. He was obsessed by one thought: the necessity of loving God and surrendering ourselves to him completely" (p. 21). Translator John Beevers very aptly summed up Jean-Pierre de Caussade in two lines. Father Caussade was born in the latter half of the seventeenth century and ordained a Jesuit priest in 1704. He took his doctorate in theology and spent time traveling France as a professor of theology. His little book, *Abandonment to Divine Providence*, was compiled after his death from letters and notes from spiritual conferences he gave to the Visitation nuns of Nancy, France. Long after his death in 1751, Father Caussade's writings continue to teach the importance of complete commitment to the will of God.

The first lines of the book, "Today God still speaks to us as he used to speak to our ancestors," are especially captivating to a modern audience (p. 22). This idea recurs several times throughout the text: Neither Caussade's generation nor our own is exceptionally different from that of the saints of the Bible; we all have access to God in the same ways. Caussade writes that God is trying to speak to us in every moment, to convey His will. It is our job to listen and obey. Caussade wrote of our biblical ancestors: "they knew only that each moment brought a duty which must be faithfully fulfilled" (p. 22). We can read holy texts, meditate, and pray, but there is nothing more important to the growth of the soul than doing what God wills in the present moment.

Part of living in the present moment is being able to recognize God's will. Caussade says that "the actions of created beings are veils which hide the profound mysteries of the workings of God" (p.36). More mystically, he continues to explain that every moment of life was crafted by God for the personal edification of the individual. God wills every experience, every second, every breath. If all moments hold importance, then we must pay close attention to better discern the will of God. Every moment in life offers boundless treasure, if we know how to grasp it. And if we believe that "there is never a moment when God does not come forward in the guise of some suffering or duty," we can happily endure trials and failures knowing that God wills them (p. 36).

At several points in the book, Caussade laments his own inability to fully abandon himself, and he later mentions the difficulty of living a passive life of self-abandonment, especially in contrast to those who seem to live active, devoted lives. Comparison is the thief of joy, and this is no less true in comparing virtues. But Caussade wrote that he who practices self-abandonment though living humbly is actually practicing every virtue. And this makes perfect sense. If God is a loving Creator who saves us from evil, who "takes the helm and brings us into port" when we are about to run onto rocks, then trusting Him is the ultimate virtue (p. 69). Doing His will with joy is expressing an attitude of "pure love, pure hope or pure faith" (p. 62).

While he sometimes complained of the difficulty of self-abandonment, Caussade's way of life also seems both meditative and comforting. Abandonment's appeal derives from its sense that it does not require intense spiritual experiences or memorization of theological tomes. In fact, Caussade made it clear that we must not try to force our own spiritual growth: "If we feel neither desire nor ability to perform marvels similar to those which make the saints so admirable, we should, in justice to ourselves, say: 'God wants these things from the saints, but not from me'" (p. 77).

In his final sections, Caussade names faith as the backbone of self-abandonment. Though this way of life might come with its own set of insecurities and humiliations, he wrote, there is truly no easier way to live. We must simply trust that God has the best intentions for us. With this in mind Caussade concludes with a meditation on earthly suffering in a few beautiful lines: "Souls who walk in light sing the hymns of light; those who walk in the shadows chant the hymns of darkness" (p. 101). Even those souls who walk in earthly darkness, Caussade wrote, will be filled with eternal light.

PASSAGES FOR REFLECTION
AND CONTEMPLATION

In reality, holiness consists of one thing only: complete loyalty to God's will. . . .

To be actively loyal means obeying the laws of God and the Church and fulfilling all the duties imposed on us by our way of life. Passive loyalty means that we lovingly accept all that God sends us at each moment of the day. (p. 24)

Holiness is produced in us by the will of God and our acceptance of it. It is not produced by intellectual speculation about it. If we are thirsty we must have a drink and not worry about books which explain what thirst is. If we waste time seeking an explanation about thirst, all that will happen is that we shall get thirstier. It is the same when we thirst after holiness. The desire to know more about it will only drive it further away. We must put all speculation aside and, with childlike willingness, accept all that God presents to us. (p. 27)

We may meditate, indulge in contemplation, pray aloud, practice interior silence, live an active life or one withdrawn from the world, and though they may all be valuable, there is nothing better for us than to do what God wants at any particular moment. (p. 30)

The actions of created beings are veils which hide the profound mysteries of the workings of God. . . . There is never a moment when God does not come forward in the guise of some suffering or duty, and all that takes place within us, around us and through us both includes and hides his activity. (p. 36)

It is faith which interprets God for us. Without its light we should not even know that God was speaking, but would hear only the confused, meaningless babble of creatures. As Moses saw the flame of fire in the bush and heard the voice of God coming from it, so faith will enable us to understand his hidden signs, so that amidst all the apparent clutter and disorder we shall see all the loveliness and perfection of divine wisdom. Faith transforms the earth into paradise. By it our hearts are raised with the joy of our nearness to heaven. Every moment reveals God to us. Faith is our light in this life. (p. 37)

Surely we must realize that in every age, including this one, God's will works through every moment, making each one holy and giving it a supernatural quality. Can we imagine that in the days of old there was a secret method of abandoning oneself to the divine will that is now out of date? And had the saints of those early times any other secret apart from that of obeying God's will from moment to moment? And will not God continue until the end of the world to pour out his grace upon all the souls who utterly abandon themselves to him? (p. 50)

This work in our souls cannot be accomplished by cleverness, intelligence, or any subtlety of mind, but only by completely abandoning ourselves to the divine action, becoming like metal poured into a mold, or a canvas waiting for the brush, or a marble under the sculptor's hands. It is surely clear that we shall not assume that image which the eternal wisdom wishes us to have by trying to understand all the mysterious activities of God down through the centuries. We can receive God's seal on our souls only by abandoning our will to him, not by any efforts of our reason. (pp. 56–57)

He cares nothing about thwarting us. If we are going eastward, he makes us turn to the west. If we are about to run onto the rocks, he takes the helm and brings us into port. We have neither map nor compass, know nothing of winds or tides, yet we always make a prosperous voyage. If pirates try to board us, an unexpected gust of wind sweeps us beyond their reach. (pp. 68–69)

Souls who walk in light sing the hymns of light; those who walk in the shadows chant the hymns of darkness. Each must be allowed to sing through to the end the words and melody which God has given him. Nothing must be changed in what he has composed. Every drop of distress, bitter as gall though it may be, must be allowed to flow, no matter what its effect on us. It was the same for Jeremiah and Ezekiel, whose every utterance was broken by sighs and tears. . . . The spirit which makes us suffer is the only one which can comfort us. These different waters flow from the same source. . . . [W]e can only let the divine project develop, for within itself it contains both the disease and its cure. So, beloved souls, weep and tremble. Remain in torment. Make no attempt to escape from these divinely inspired terrors. Receive in the depths of your hearts the little streams which flow from the sea of sorrow which filled the most holy soul of Jesus. Keep advancing and let your tears flow under the influence of grace. This same influence will finally dry your eyes. The clouds will drift away, the sun will shine again, spring will adorn you with its flowers, and then you will see, because of your abandonment, the full extent of what the divine action is accomplishing. (pp. 101–102)

[T]he simplest sermons, the most ordinary conversations and the most trivial books can become, through God's will, sources of knowledge and wisdom. This is why self-abandoned souls always carefully gather up the crumbs which the proud tread underfoot, for everything is precious to them and there is nothing which does not enrich them. (p. 106)

DISCUSSION QUESTIONS

1. In the first section of the book, Caussade writes about active and passive loyalty. "To be passively loyal is even easier, since it implies only that we accept what very often we cannot avoid, and endure with love and resignation things which could cause us weariness and disgust" (p. 25). What is the difference between active and passive loyalty? Is it true that passive loyalty is easier to accomplish?

2. Caussade says that God's action can only fill our souls if "we empty them of all false confidence in our own ability." What implications does this awareness of one's limitations have for a soul trying to live humbly? How is "knowing thyself" important to fulfilling God's intentions for you?

3. Section 8 of the second chapter discusses the idea that every moment is important because it was meant for us personally, and that "[w]e can understand nothing perfectly except what experience has taught through what we have suffered and done" (p. 49). How does

this idea of constant, personally intended moments alter your idea of how we grow in wisdom?

4. "Neither reason nor the senses are ever satisfied, for they never see the sufficiency of grace" (p. 51). If reason cannot see the sufficiency of grace, then how do we overcome reason to better appreciate God's grace?

5. At one point, the author compares the life of self-abandonment to "becoming like metal poured into a mold" (p. 56). A little later he laments that he has not yet himself "been cast into the mold designed for me" (p. 57). How does Caussade's admission change the tone of the book, if at all? What does this say about the nature of the pursuit of a life of God?

6. "Some of us will live in the shadows and some of us in the full light of day" writes Caussade (p. 63). Later on in the book, he speaks both of God always taking care of us, and God allowing constant struggles in our lives. All these ideas seem paradoxical, that God both allows some of us to walk in shadow, some in light, but ultimately loves and provides for all of us. How can we reconcile these truths?

7. Caussade writes that the person living a life of self-abandonment is like a block of marble, and God is the sculptor who chips away at the marble to reveal the image He has in mind. But the block must trust that it will eventually be a masterpiece. What uncertain circumstances in your life have you resolved to let go and trust that things would work out? What have you learned from accepting hardship, rather than trying to control outcomes?

8. At the conclusion of his fifth chapter, Caussade writes: "Finally, after several transformations, the formed and finished soul, now endowed with wings, flies up to heaven" (p. 98). Do you feel that your own soul has gone through a significant transformation at any given time? What implications does this statement have as to the author's belief in providence and God's will?

9. The author writes that self-abandoned souls can experience debility or weakness, but that this is all part of God's plan. "These souls should carry on cheerfully along the road, ignoring all the suffering that God sends them" (p. 111). The author often describes the value not only of doing God's will faithfully, but of doing it with joy. Is the attitude with which something is done more important than the doing? Has approaching a negative situation with a positive outlook ever changed the outcome?

10. "There is nothing more prudent than to offer no resistance to one's enemies and face them in simple self-abandonment" (p. 109). It seems that the answer to most problems, according to de Caussade, is living the life of self-abandonment. How would living a life of self-abandonment look to you?